OUR
BEST
COOKBOOK

A collection of fine recipes submitted by members of the Wisconsin Restaurant Association.

Edited by Rita C. Schultz

First Edition

Library of Congress Catalog Number: 93-61498
ISBN: 0-942495-31-4

Wisconsin Restaurant Association
Education Foundation
31 South Henry Street, # 300
Madison, Wisconsin 53703

For additional copies of this book contact:
Amherst Press
318 N. Main Street
P.O. Box 296
Amherst, WI 54406
or call 1-800-333-8122

Printed in USA by
Palmer Publications, Inc.
Amherst, WI 54406

Table of Contents

Wisconsin Restaurant Association Education Foundation 1993 Board of Directors

Acknowledgements

Warm thanks are due to the following for support that helped make this book possible.

The Board of Directors of the Wisconsin Restaurant Association Education Foundation provided the inspiration to bring this project to fruition.

Our contributing restaurateurs long believed in our effort and underwrote our project. Their generousity benefits us all.

Walter Mazur, owner/chef of the Blue Bayou Inn, Manitowish Waters, gave us the original idea and contributed his promotional expertise.

Special thanks to Kurt Pare of Nationwide Menus, La Crosse, for his dedication and generousity. His early efforts spirited us on to complete this book. We owe him a debt of gratitude.

Denise Thompson and Nathan Lump, associates at the Wisconsin Restaurant Association Education Foundation, did the initial systems work with dedication and humor. Their efforts allowed us to maintain our production schedule.

Scholarships in Foodservice

Proceeds from the sale of this book will go towards the Wisconsin Restaurant Association Education Foundation Scholarship Program.

Each year the Education Foundation awards scholarships of $500 or $1,000 to twenty or more students. These students are training in a variety of foodservice career paths. They may be enrolled in a one-, two-, or four-year program. The student must be employed in a Wisconsin foodservice position at the time of application.

The Education Foundation also participates in a special needs scholarship program for foodservice students through the vocational technical colleges. Other grants and support are given as the need arises; such as money donated to help the Future Homemakers of America Home Economics Related Occupations (FHA-HERO) students attend their national conferences. Since 1983, the Foundation has awarded over $130,000 in scholarships, grants and aids.

Anyone interested in this program or other Education Foundation endeavors is welcome to contact Sally Scott, Managing Director; 800-589-3211.

Introduction

There are few subjects of greater interest than food. And whether the purpose is social or business, to celebrate or to mourn, we have come to expect the presence of food whenever we come together.

So it is with great pleasure that the Wisconsin Restaurant Association Education Foundation presents OUR BEST COOKBOOK, a collection of the finest recipes from some of Wisconsin's finest restaurants.

Conceived of by the Education Foundation's Board of Directors, the purpose of this project is twofold: to do honor to the rich tradition of Wisconsin's hospitality industry, and to provide scholarships for individuals wishing to pursue careers in the field of foodservice.

Within these pages you will discover some of Wisconsin's best restaurants, get a glimpse of their personal histories, and have a chance to enjoy their superb and varied menus in the relaxed intimacy of your home.

Or you may choose to use this volume as a travel guide. A stop at any or all of these restaurants is sure to nourish both body and spirit, making your excursions throughout the state more memorable. See the 'Map' for restaurants and communities represented.

Many of us would agree that life comes down to a few simple things. Certainly food and fine dining offer us one of life's simple, but great pleasures. We at the Wisconsin Restaurant Association Education Foundation are pleased to contribute OUR BEST COOKBOOK towards this end. We know that you will enjoy it.

Rita C. Schultz

Rita C. Schultz
Education Programs Coordinator

OUR BEST COOKBOOK

Contributing Members and Their Recipes

Guide to Contributing Members' Restaurants

1 **Appleton**—TrimB's
2 **Bayfield**—Old Rittenhouse Inn
3 **Brookfield**—Cafe Vienna
4 **Cudahy**—Fountain Blue
5 **Delavan**—Millie's Restaurants
6 **Dodgeville**—Thym's Supper Club
7 **Eau Claire**—The Brothers Three; Fanny Hill Restaurant, Inn & Dinner Theatre
8 **Ellison Bay**—Grandma's Swedish Restaurant
9 **Green Bay**—Rock Garden Supper Club
10 **Hudson**—Dick's Bar and Grill
11 **King**—King's Table Restaurant
12 **Kohler**—The American Club, The Horse & Plow Restaurant
13 **Lake Geneva**—The Grandview Restaurant & Lounge
14 **Lomira**—Bublitz's Family Restaurant
15 **Madison**—Kavanaugh's Esquire Club; Quivey's Grove
16 **Manitowish Waters**—The Blue Bayou Inn Restaurant
17 **Marinette**—The Brothers Three
18 **Marshfield**—Belvedere Supper Club
19 **Mequon**—Boder's on the River; Chancery Pub and Restaurant
20 **Milwaukee**—Bodolino's Pizza Restaurant; Chancery Pub and Restaurant; The Clock Steak House; Friendly Inn Supper Club, Inc.; Grenadier's Restaurant; Karl Ratzsch's Old World Restaurant; Mader's Restaurant; Marc's Cafe and Coffee Mill; Pasta! basta!; The Pfister Hotel, The Cafe; The Pfister Hotel, The English Room; Weissgerber's Third Street Pier
21 **Minoqua**—Polecat & Lace
22 **Mountain**—Tailgate Resort Motel
23 **Neenah**—The Valley Inn
24 **New Glarus**—New Glarus Hotel
25 **Oconto**—The Brothers Three
26 **Oshkosh**—Butch's Anchor Inn
27 **Osseo**—Norske Nook
28 **Pewaukee**—Western Lakes Golf Club
29 **Portage**—Blankenhaus of Good Food
30 **Prescott**—Steamboat Inn
31 **Racine**—Chancery Pub and Restaurant
32 **Stevens Point**—Bernard's
33 **Waukesha**—Chancery Pub and Restaurant
34 **Wausau**—2510 Restaurant
35 **Wauwatosa**—Chancery Pub and Restaurant
36 **Whitefish Bay**—Jack Pandl's Whitefish Bay Inn
37 **Wisconsin Dells**—Dick's Polish-American Smorgasbord

Map XI

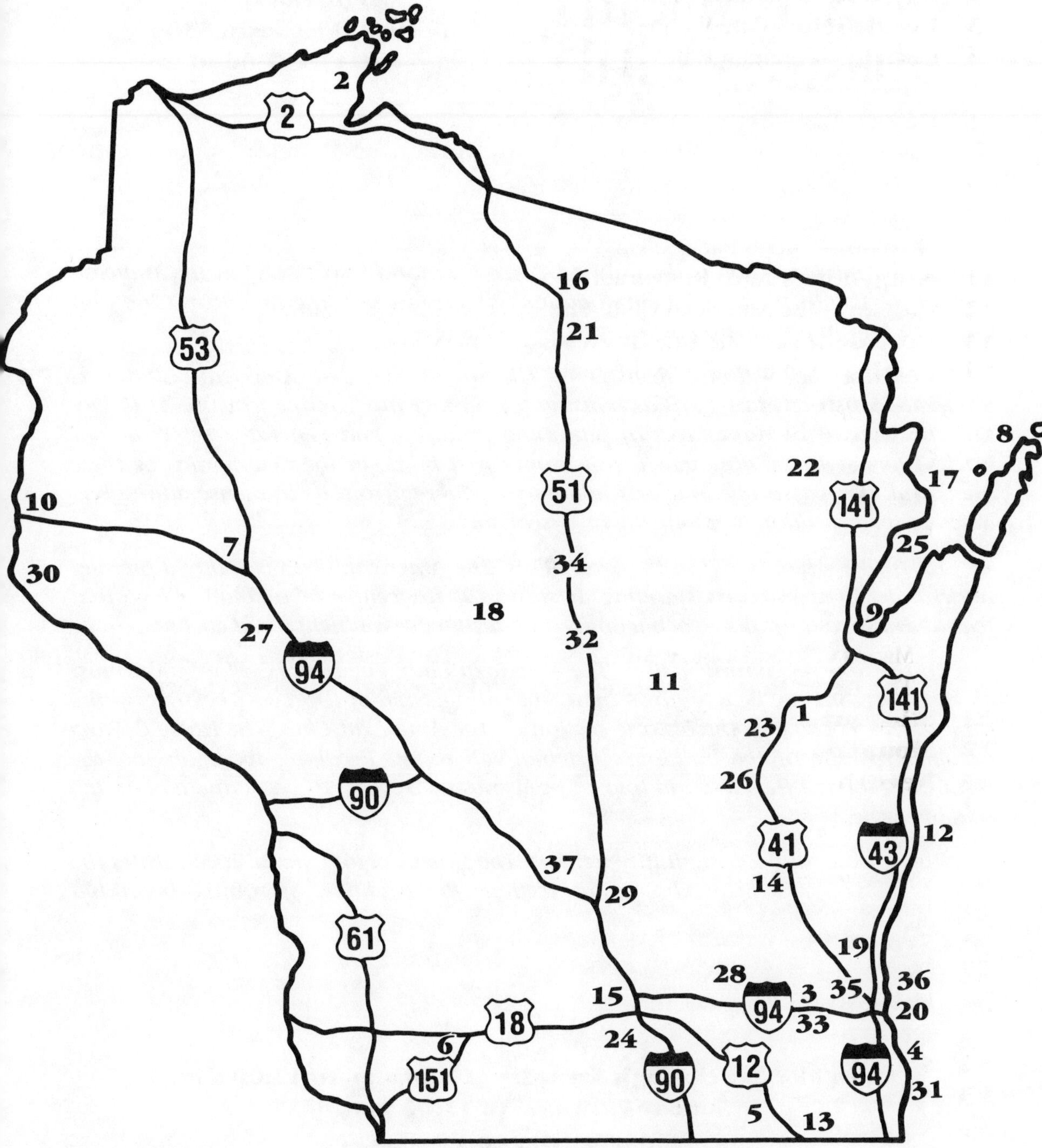
2
2
53
16
21
51
22
141
8
17
10
7
30
25
34
18
9
27
94
32
11
141
1
23
26
90
41
43
12
37
14
29
61
19
28
36
15
94
3
35
20
33
18
24
6
4
90
12
94
151
31
5
13

The American Club
The Horse & Plow Restaurant
Highland Drive
Kohler, Wisconsin 53044
(414) 457-8000

The American Club is the only AAA Five Diamond resort hotel in the Midwest. Known for its outstanding accommodations and amenities, The American Club also has a reputation for superb cuisine.

Listed on the National Register of Historic Places, The American Club was originally constructed in 1918 as housing for immigrants coming to work at Kohler Co., the leading manufacturer of plumbing products and generator sets. The red brick, Tudor-style building was a welcoming first home in the new world for these men. And, the reassuring smells of home-style cooking from its immense dining hall aided in the transition to a new life in Wisconsin.

Extensively remodeled in the late 1970s, The American Club is today a premier resort hotel of world-class standing. It stands at the center of a small village that features nine restaurants—each with its own distinctive ambience and cuisine.

Of the four restaurants within The American Club, The Horse & Plow is the most casual—presenting hearty fare in a charming turn-of-the century tavern-like atmosphere. Located in the historic section of The American Club, The Horse & Plow occupies the site of the building's original tap room. Recalling those origins, the restaurant today offers a world tour of breweries with scores of beers and ales on tap and by bottle.

This cheese soup is a signature item on The Horse & Plow menu. It celebrates the rich flavors of Wisconsin cheeses, as well as the tradition of robust, heartland cooking.

Open Monday through Saturday, 11:30 a.m. to 12:00 a.m.
Sunday 7:00 a.m. to 11:00 p.m.

All major credit cards accepted

Wisconsin Three Cheese Soup

½ pound butter
2 cups diced onions
2 tablespoons chopped fresh garlic
½ cup flour
2 quarts milk
2 bay leaves
½ pound shredded Wisconsin jalapeno jack cheese
½ pound shredded Wisconsin cheddar cheese
½ pound shredded Wisconsin Swiss cheese
Salt to taste
Black pepper to taste
Dash nutmeg
1 12-ounce bottle of Wisconsin beer

In a 1½ gallon soup pot, melt butter; sauté onions and garlic until tender. Add flour; mix well. Cook for 5 minutes, stirring frequently over medium heat. Add milk. Whip with a whisk to blend in milk. Add bay leaves. Cook over low heat for 20 minutes, stirring constantly.

Stir in cheeses, in one direction only until thoroughly mixed and cheese is melted. Season with salt, pepper and nutmeg. Stir in beer and serve.

Yields 12-14 servings.

Belvedere Supper Club
M329 Highway 97
Marshfield, Wisconsin 54449
(715) 387-4161

The Belvedere Supper Club is located on Highway 97, three miles north of Marshfield and six miles south of Stratford, Wisconsin.

The Leffel family has been in the restaurant business since 1934. Pat and Dale Leffel built the Belvedere Supper Club in 1984, and have since added a large reception hall with private bar, and a smaller private dining and meeting room.

Lovely weddings can be held at our outdoor chapel found on the beautiful grounds also.

The Belvedere is a full-service restaurant, caters weddings, parties, business meetings, and sponsors tours to various locations. Carry-out is also available.

"It has always been a family tradition to make you feel at home and we welcome your visit anytime."

Open 7 days a week
Noon lunch Monday through Friday, 11:00 a.m. to 2:00 p.m.
Saturday open at 4:00 p.m.
Sunday Brunch 10:00 a.m. to 2:00 p.m.
and from 2:00 p.m. to 10:00 p.m. open menu

All major credit cards accepted

German Potato Salad

1 pound potatoes
2 strips bacon
1½ tablespoons chopped onion
2 tablespoons water
3 tablespoons sugar
¼ cup vinegar
¾ scant teaspoon cornstarch
Salt to taste

Cook potatoes with peels left on until tender. Peel and slice or dice into a pan or crock pot.

Chop bacon into small pieces. Brown in a frying pan over medium heat. Remove cooked bacon from pan. Add onion to bacon drippings, sautéing until tender.

Add water, sugar, and vinegar. Thicken with cornstarch. Salt to taste.

Heat on low heat in crock pot, oven or in a very large frying pan.

Yields approximately 4-6 servings.

Bernard's
701 Second Street North
Stevens Point, Wisconsin 54481
(715) 344-3365

Superb Dining in the Old World Atmosphere

Bernard Kurzawa, the genius behind Bernard's (who else?), was apprenticed to a chef in Germany when he was 14 years old. Today Bernard is a true chef de cuisine with 41 years of experience under his belt. Says he "Food is different all the time; it's not calibrated by any machine. So if you want to be a good chef you have to be able to make the proper adjustments in your cooking, cutting and mixing."

Diners at Bernard's, just north of Stevens Point, agree that he makes the proper adjustments. Just try a jaeger schnitzel, holsteiner schnitzel or the zigeuner schnitzel, each a savory variation on the wiener schnitzel theme. The duck l'orange is as good as the duck German-style, which is smothered in gravy and served with potato dumplings. After dinner treats include the famous Black Forest torte, the blackberry-port sorbet, hot apple strudel and fresh roasted coffee.

Bernard loves to do chef demo's for groups of twenty or more and people love to eat the finished product.

Bernard's is out in the country a bit and resembles one of the area's many barns, but under the roof is a white-linen atmosphere and casual dining.

Open from 4:00 p.m.
Seven days a week
Banquet facilities from 25 to 500 people

Diner's Club, VISA, Discover,
Carte Blanc, MasterCard accepted

Zigeuner Schnitzel

(Gypsy Steak)

2 pounds centercut boneless porkloin
2 tablespoons butter or vegetable shortening
Flour to coat
1 cup sliced mushrooms
½ cup finely chopped onions
½ cup diced smoked bacon
1 cup dry white wine
2 tablespooons tomato paste
1 teaspoon hot Hungarian paprika
Salt to taste

Trim porkloin of all visible fat and silverskin. Cut porkloin into four equal parts and butterfly. Using the flat part of a cleaver or a meat mallet, pound steaks to ¼ inch thick.

Heat butter in 12-inch heavy skillet over medium heat. Flour the steaks, and lightly sauté until almost done. Remove from skillet. Set aside.

Turn heat to high and sauté mushrooms, onions and bacon in the same skillet. Add white wine, tomato paste, paprika and salt. Let simmer and reduce for three minutes. Return pork to sauce and reheat.

Chef's Note: This meat should be served with Spatzel, dumpling or your favorite pasta. If hot Hungarian paprika is not available, substitute Spanish paprika and add a few drops of Tabasco sauce.

Yields 4 servings.

Blankenhaus
The Haus of Good Food
cocktails dancing

Blankenhaus of Good Food
1223 East Wisconsin
Highway 51 South at edge of town
Portage, Wisconsin 53901
(608) 742-7555

A Portage landmark, known in years past as "The Roost," was acquired by the Blankenheim family in 1978. Extensive remodeling to the building followed and it was reopened in 1979 as The Blankenhaus. The name was taken from the German name "Blankenheim" which means clean or white home.

Today this popular dining spot is operated by Jim and Kay Blankenheim who took over the well-known restaurant in 1985 from Jim's parents, Romie and Pauline Blankenheim.

Jim, Kay and the entire staff constantly work to improve and fine-tune the business to meet the ever changing tastes of their customers who come from far and wide to enjoy the ambiance and tasty cuisine.

The Blankenhaus has long been a gathering place for family and friends, class reunions, birthdays, anniversaries, business meetings, clubs and tour buses.

Thanks to past and present employees and our wonderful and loyal customers, the restaurant has been the recipient of several awards over the years. The Blankenhaus is dedicated to paying close attention to detail, food and service in a thoroughly friendly and comfortable atmosphere so it will remain one of the favorite gathering places in the area.

Open Tuesday through Thursday,
Lunch 11 a.m to 2 p.m., Dinner 4:30 p.m. to 10 p.m.
Friday Lunch 11 a.m. to 2 p.m.
Friday and Saturday, Dinner 4:30 p.m. to 11 p.m.
Sunday Brunch (Buffet) 11 a.m. to 2 p.m.
Sunday Dinner (off menu) 2 p.m. to 10 p.m.

MasterCard and Visa accepted

Blankenhaus Chocolate Torte

½ pound butter, softened
2 cups powdered sugar
2 squares unsweetened chocolate, melted, cooled
¼ cup evaporated milk
1 8-ounce container whipped topping or 1 cup cream, whipped
1 cup chopped walnuts
1 cup finely ground graham cracker crumbs
Whipped topping or whipped cream, for garnish

Cream butter and sugar with electric mixer. Blend in chocolate. Add milk and blend. Fold in whipped topping or cream, along with nuts.

Dust bottom of 9x13-inch ungreased pan with graham cracker crumbs, then spread chocolate mixture into pan. Freeze 1 to 2 hours, or until firm.

Garnish with whipped topping when ready to serve.

Chef's Note: For a party dessert, multiply everything by four. Use a large sheet pan, sprinkle with graham cracker crumbs, add mixture and freeze. Top each piece with a swirl of whipped topping.

Yields 12 servings.

The Blue Bayou Inn Restaurant
U.S. 51 at the Spider Lake Bridge
Manitowish Waters, Wisconsin 54545
(715) 543-2537

The Blue Bayou Inn—a restaurant that has truly set itself apart from the others in the Northwoods! Through the efforts of Chef Walt Mazur, his wife Rita, his family, and a fine staff—The Blue Bayou Inn has become one of the finest restaurants in the Northwoods—if not in the entire state of Wisconsin.

Chef Walter, having been trained in the kitchens of Louisiana, brought Louisiana cookery to the state of Wisconsin via the Northwoods of Manitowish Waters. The Blue Bayou has distinguished itself as something of a dining legend by way of its authentic cuisine and captivating atmosphere.

The Blue Bayou Inn received a 4-star rating by the Milwaukee Journal in 1988; has been honored by accolades in Wisconsin Trails Magazine, The Chicago Tribune, and numerous other publications. The Blue Bayou Inn and Chef Mazur have been awarded a three diamond rating by AAA; and "Restaurateur of The Year" by his peers of the Northwoods Chapter of The Wisconsin Restaurant Association.

Real Louisiana food is a symphony of flavor that requires a maestro's hand in seasoning and preparation. Only a few restaurants have taken Louisiana cooking seriously, and The Blue Bayou is one. Mazur's menu features specialties learned from Louisiana chefs—Crawfish or Shrimp Etoufee, Bayou Kitchen Jambalaya, and Catfish served six different ways, to name just a few.

A favorite of many is the Angler's Special: "Bring in the fish you caught today and we'll prepare it just the way you like," promises Chef Walt. In addition to Louisiana cuisine, The Blue Bayou's extensive menu includes all-American fare as well. You'll also find an excellent selection of appetizers, soups and salads. One shouldn't overlook the authentic southern desserts that will tantalize any sweet-tooth. If you'd enjoy a cocktail, you'll find your favorite in the Steamboat Lounge.

Open Monday-Saturday and Holiday weekends
Late April through October
Steamboat Lounge 3:30 p.m.
Dinner 5:00 p.m. to 10:30 p.m.
Lunch by reservation only - (800) 533-9671
Wheelchair accessible — Non-smoking available

Visa, Discover, MasterCard accepted

Shrimp Victoria

16 large shrimp, 16-20 count
Louisiana Hot Sauce
Sea salt to taste
¼ cup sweet unsalted butter
½ cup chopped green onions
1 cup sliced mushrooms
⅓ cup white wine, Chablis preferred
1 tablespoon whole wheat flour
⅓ cup sour cream
1 cup natural brown rice, cooked
1 tablespoon finely chopped parsley, for garnish

Peel shrimp leaving tail on. Place in small bowl. Cover with Louisiana Hot Sauce and a pinch of salt. Set aside and let shrimp marinate for about 5 minutes.

In a large sauté pan, melt butter until slightly brown, add green onions, sauté for 1 minute, then add mushrooms. Sauté for 2 more minutes, then add shrimp and white wine. Lower heat to simmer. Wait 2 minutes, then add flour. Simmer for about 4-5 minutes, stirring occasionally. Sauce will thicken.

Add sour cream 1 minute before serving. Mix in thoroughly. Serve over or with rice on the side. Garnish with parsley.

Chef's Note: Always buy shrimp with shell on. That is the best way to buy and will give you the best flavor!

Yields 2 servings.

Boder's on the River
11919 North River Road 43 West
Mequon, Wisconsin 53092
(414) 242-0335

Owned and Operated by
The Boder Family Since 1929

Way back in 1929, the Boder family decided to serve only the best of everything, and plenty of it, a tradition which has continued these many years. All of the relishes, muffins, dressings, fritters, and desserts are prepared in our own kitchen; that way we know they are the best.

Today, the restaurant is owned and operated by the third generation of the Boder family: Jean Fisher, John and Nancy Walch, and Fred and Mary Krautkramer. Jack and Dolly Boder, who bought the restaurant in 1954 from Jack's parents, John and Frieda, are still active in the business when they are at home in Mequon.

Open Tuesday through Sunday, 11:30 a.m. to 2:00 p.m.
Tuesday through Friday, 5:30 p.m. to 8:00 p.m.
Saturday 5:30 p.m. to 9:30 p.m.
Sunday 4:00 p.m. to 7:00 p.m.

All major credit cards accepted

Boder's Corn Fritters

Boder's original recipe served for over forty years

2 cups flour, sifted
1 teaspoon salt
6 teaspoons baking powder
1 tablespoon corn oil
1½ teaspoons vinegar
1 cup milk
3 eggs, separated
1 cup niblet corn, drained
Shortening
Powdered sugar
Maple syrup

Sift dry ingredients together. Add corn oil, vinegar, milk, egg yolks, and corn. Mix well—mixture should be moist, not dry. Fold in stiffly beaten egg whites.

Fill deep skillet with shortening (fresh shortening is necessary). Melt to 350 degrees. Drop large spoonfuls of batter into shortening. Deep fry until golden brown.

Place finished fritter in muffin tin and bake in oven at 325 degrees for 10 minutes.

Sprinkle with powdered sugar and serve with maple syrup.

Chef's Note: An electric frying pan may be used to deep fry fritters.

Yields 6-8 fritters.

Bodolino's PIZZA RESTAURANT

Bodolino's Pizza Restaurant
3124 North Downer Avenue
Milwaukee, Wisconsin 53211
(414) 964-9616

For pizza beyond compare, dine in or carry out at Bobolino's, the casual and affordable place for pizza on Milwaukee's east side.

Bodolino's unforgettable pizzas start with a thick, chewy, delicious crust. Then come the toppings. For those craving a traditional pizza, Bobolino's serves their own tantalizing tomato sauce with your favorite toppings. The more adventurous will find something to their liking, too. Try your favorite toppings on one of a variety of sauces or maybe you would like to try a customer favorite such as spinach pesto with feta cheese or artichokes with roasted garlic.

Bodolino's also serves appetizers, sandwiches, daily soups and weekly specials.

Serving starting at 10:30 a.m.
Monday through Saturday

All major credit cards accepted

Mc Jack Pepper Turkey Pita

4 pitas, Greek-style or whole wheat
20-24 ounces smoked turkey breast, sliced
1 red onion, thinly sliced
2 unpeeled McIntosh apples, thinly sliced
16 slices Monterey Jack cheese
Fresh black pepper
4-6 ounces alfalfa sprouts

Place pitas flat on baking sheet. Top each pita with equal amounts of turkey slices, ruffling turkey so that it stands up. Place equal amounts of onion on top of turkey. Arrange apple slices in circular pattern on each pita; top with cheese slices.

Bake at 375 degrees until meat is hot and cheese melted, approximately 10-15 minutes.

Dust pitas with pepper and top with sprouts. Quarter pitas and serve.

Chef's Note: This sandwich is excellent served with additional apple wedges and chips or fresh vegetables. Makes a savory appetizer too!

Yields 4 servings.

the brothers three for hungry people

The Brothers Three
1720 Harding Avenue
Eau Claire, Wisconsin 54701
(715) 839-7322

The Brothers three was established in Cicero, Illinois in January 1968. Three brothers, Glen, Keith and Dale Nergaard, formed a corporation and started out as a "Shakey's Pizza" franchise.

Over the years the stores have thrived and there have been numerous expansions. Today, the Brothers Three operate stores in Eau Claire, Marinette and Oconto.

As the stores grew, sandwiches were added to the menu followed by full lunch and dinner selections. The Eau Claire store also serves breakfast, and all three stores have full liquor licenses.

The Nergaard brothers celebrated 25 years in the business this year.

Open seven days a week
6 a.m. to 10 p.m.

All major credit cards accepted

Cranberry Pumpkin Muffins

- **4 eggs**
- **1 cup vegetable oil**
- **4 cups sugar**
- **2½ cups canned pumpkin**
- **2 cups sliced fresh or frozen cranberries**
- **4½ cups all-purpose flour**
- **2¼ tablespoon pumpkin pie spice**
- **1 teaspoon salt**
- **2 teaspoons baking soda**

Mix eggs, oil, sugar, pumpkin and cranberries together. In a separate bowl, mix flour, pumpkin pie spice, salt and baking soda together. Combine wet and dry ingredients, taking care not to overmix.

Scoop batter into muffin liners about ¾ full. Bake at 375 degrees until done—toothpick will come out clean. Internal muffin temperature should be 180 degrees.

Yields 24 regular or 12 jumbo muffins.

the brothers three for hungry people

The Brothers Three
1302 Marinette Avenue
Marinette, Wisconsin 54143
(715) 735-9054

The Brothers Three in Marinette opened May 19, 1971 and is still growing. Over this period of time, we have had six major expansions. What was once a small neighborhood tavern is now the restaurant you see today. We take pride in our fast, courteous service, as well as our quality food. Although we serve the "finest" pizza in northern Wisconsin, we also serve a wide variety of appetizers, sandwiches, dinner plates and desserts. The entire family can dine in one place and still satisfy everyone's appetite.

The Brothers Three was first established in Cicero, Illinois in 1968. We had originally been a Shakey's franchise but broke ties with them to become more independent and to develop our own recipes. In the 1970's we expanded our locations into Wisconsin and at the present have locations in Marinette, Oconto, and Eau Claire. The Marinette restaurant is the largest of our current operations. Our staff of over forty employees extends a warm welcome to you.

Open Monday through Thursday, 11 a.m. to 11 p.m.
Friday and Saturday, 11 a.m. to 12 a.m.

MasterCard, Visa, and Discover accepted

Karen's Tender Mexican Chili

8 ounces tomato puree
1 tablespoon beef base
6 ounces beer
1 13-ounce can diced green chilies
1½ tablespoons kitchen bouquet
3 tablespoons chili powder
1 teaspoon oregano
1 tablespoon cumin, ground
2 bay leaves
½ level teaspoon cayenne red pepper
½ tablespoon sugar
1 teaspoon black pepper
Salt to taste
2 - 2½ pounds tenderloin pieces
2 large onions, finely chopped
2 garlic cloves, finely chopped
Cooking oil
3 16-ounce cans Mexican style chili beans, drained
12 ounces shredded sharp cheddar cheese
Sour cream, optional

In a large Dutch oven, combine tomato puree, beef base, beer, green chilies, kitchen bouquet, chili powder, oregano, cumin, bay leaves, cayenne red pepper, sugar, black pepper, and salt. Simmer while preparing other items.

Cut tenderloin into small cubes. In a large pan, sauté tenderloin cubes, diced onions (reserving some raw for garnish), and garlic in hot cooking oil. Add to liquid mixture, simmer for 1½ hours, and stir in beans.

Prior to serving, top with reserved raw onion, sharp cheddar cheese, and, if desired, sour cream. This is a meal in itself.

Yields 12 servings.

the brothers three *for hungry people*

The Brothers Three
106 Superior Avenue
Oconto, Wisconsin 54153
(414) 834-3471

The Brothers Three in Oconto is a full-service restaurant located on the Oconto River, specializing in pizzas made from scratch, Mexican entrees, and fine cocktails. Our cocktail lounge offers a scenic view of the Oconto River, with boat docking available. An outside deck provides dining enjoyment during the summer months. Wisconsin lottery tickets are sold here.

Our dining room features a newly-decorated private room, perfect for your banquets, private meetings, showers, or other occasions. We take pride in the variety of services we offer, such as birthday parties for pre-schoolers to pre-teens, excellent luncheon service, and senior citizen discounts.

We suggest our daily soup-and-sandwich special on our home-baked breads and rolls for your noon-hour enjoyment. Please the family with our large pizza-and-pitcher of soda special on Thursdays or with our mouth-watering fish frys on Fridays. Enjoy casual dining at its best on Saturday nights with your choice of a delicious stir-fry or a chicken dinner with all of the trimmings on Sundays. We offer noon-hour delivery service to your home or place of business and full delivery service after 4:30 p.m. daily. We are ready to handle any request to cater to your company meeting or employee picnic. Banquet and catering menus are available on request. We pride ourselves on offering the best in food and courteous service.

We celebrated 12 years of service on March 17, 1993. The Brothers Three is pleased to have made Oconto its home for these past 12 years. We suffered a fire in our early stages, but re-opened the next day due to the tremendous cooperation from the people of Oconto. We look forward to many years of service in the future.

Open seven days a week, 11 a.m. to 12 a.m.

Mastercard, Visa, Discover accepted

Steak or Chicken Fajita

Meat Marinade:
1½ cups soy sauce
2 teaspoons Lawry's seasoning
2 teaspoons garlic salt
2 teaspoons black pepper
2 tablespoons oregano
12 ounces steak or chicken, cubed

Fajita:
Oil to cook
1 large onion, cut ¼ inch thick, julienne-style
1 green pepper, cut ¼ inch thick, julienne-style
2 tomatoes, cut in ½ inch thick wedges
4 flat pitas, whole wheat or white
1 cup shredded lettuce
4 ounces shredded cheddar cheese
1 cup guacamole
1 cup sour cream
Red or green cherry peppers, for garnish

To prepare marinade, mix all ingredients together and pour over meat. Mix thoroughly and cover. Marinate overnight in refrigerator.

To prepare marinated meat, sauté in oil in skillet for approximately 3 minutes, tossing meat to brown all sides. Add onions and green peppers and sauté 2 minutes longer. Add tomatoes and toss to combine. Sauté until heated, for approximately 1 minute.

Warm pitas on grill with a little oil on both sides. Place meat and vegetables in each pita, fold top side over, and secure each with wooden picks.

Serve lettuce topped with shredded cheddar cheese on the side to assemble to each individual taste. Serve guacamole and sour cream in 2-ounce cups on the side. Garnish with red or green cherry pepper.

Chef's Note: For steak fajitas, use sirloin tips. Be sure they are tenderized! For chicken fajitas, use only boneless, skinless, chicken breasts. This plate makes a very colorful presentation!

Yields 4 servings.

Bublitz's Family Restaurant
580 East Avenue Hwys 41 and 67
Lomira, Wisconsin 53048
(414) 269-4010

For 10 years the Bublitz family has been in the food service business, currently owning three restaurants. Bublitz's Family Restaurant, located in Lomira, features outstanding buffets, served both at noon and in the evening, offering a variety of dishes, breads and soups to please any palate.

Located near Horicon Marsh, Bublitz's Family Restaurants welcomes you to stop by for traditional favorites in a casual family atmosphere.

Open seven days a week
Winter hours: 6 a.m. to 8 p.m.
Summer hours: 5:30 a.m. to 9 p.m.

MasterCard, Visa, and American Express accepted

Crabby Brunch Soufflé

8 slices white bread, trimmed and diced
2 cups crab meat
½ cup mayonnaise
1 medium onion, diced
1 cup celery, diced
1 medium green pepper, diced
2 cups grated cheddar cheese, divided
2 cups milk
4 eggs, beaten
Paprika, for garnish

Place half of the bread cubes in a greased 12x8x2-inch casserole dish. In a separate bowl, mix together crab meat, mayonnaise, onion, celery, pepper, 1½ cups cheese, milk, eggs, and remaining bread cubes. Pour over bread in dish.

Garnish top with remaining ½ cup cheese and a few sprinkles of paprika. Refrigerate overnight.

Bake 1 hour in 350-degree oven.

Yields 8 servings.

Butch's Anchor Inn
225 West 20th Street
Oshkosh, Wisconsin 54903
(414) 236-5360

Butch's Anchor Inn is a family-owned and operated restaurant featuring mouth-watering seafood and steaks, homemade bread, a luncheon salad bar, and a buffet seven days each week. Private huts for dining accommodate from two to eight people. Butch's has antique nautical decor and five large ocean aquariums, including an 800-gallon shark tank. The restaurant also has banquet facilities for private parties up to 150 people. Butch's incorporated "The Italian Underground" (located below Butch's) in May of 1992. The Underground serves very fine pasta dishes, many unique signature pizzas, steaks, and sandwiches. Casual and moderately priced, The Underground offers great atmosphere.

We pride ourselves on bringing quality and excellence to you. For four generations, the Arps family has been bringing you their tradition. Great things happen when people dedicated to the restaurant industry join forces and that we do.

John "Butch" Arps, Sr. is a certified executive chef. He is a graduate of the Culinary Institute of 1960. Son John Arps, Jr. is a 1990 graduate of the Culinary Institute in Hyde Park, New York. He has been cooking for the past twelve years. Son Mike Arps is a certified apprentice chef and has been cooking for the past nine years. The culinary touch and flair is definitely in their blood.

Together our family and the entire team at Butch's Anchor Inn extend a warm welcome to all of our customers, past and new.

Open Monday through Thursday, 11 a.m. to 10 p.m.
Friday and Saturday, 11 a.m. to 11 p.m.
Sunday 10 a.m. to 10 p.m.

All major credit cards accepted

Chicken Amaretto

- **½ cup all purpose flour**
- **¼ teaspoon salt**
- **¼ teaspoon black pepper**
- **¼ teaspoon garlic powder**
- **6 tablespoons butter, divided**
- **2 5-ounce chicken breasts, boned and pounded**
- **½ cup Amaretto liquor**
- **¼ cup almonds**
- **¼ cup pecans**
- **2 cups white rice**
- **Strawberry fan or kiwi star, for garnish**

Combine flour, salt, pepper, and garlic powder in a self-sealing bag or on a plate. Set aside.

Melt 3 tablespoons butter in a medium sauce pan, over medium heat. Lightly dredge chicken breasts in flour mixture. Place in pan. Cook for exactly 2 minutes per side. Remove to heated platter.

Add Amaretto to pan and reduce by half. Add almonds and pecans. Then add remaining 3 tablespoons of butter to caramelize the sauce for 1 to 2 minutes. Pour sauce over chicken. Serve over white rice along with a vegetable (perhaps baby carrots or broccoli). Garnish with strawberry fan or kiwi star.

Yields 2-4 servings.

Lowe

Pan Fried Pike
with Pecan Sauce

1 cup all purpose flour
¼ teaspoon salt
¼ teaspoon black pepper
⅛ teaspoon garlic powder
5 tablespoons unsalted butter, divided
2 8-10 ounce pike fillets
1 cup cup coarsely chopped pecans
¼ cup dry white wine, preferably chablis
2 cups heavy whipping cream
Juice of half a lemon
1 teaspoon brown sugar
Lemon twist, for garnish

Combine flour, salt, pepper, and garlic powder on a plate. Set aside.

In a large sauté pan, melt 3 tablespoons of butter over medium heat. Dredge pike fillets lightly in flour mixture. Place in pan, skin side up (this helps to reduce curling and shrinkage of fillet). Sauté until golden brown, carefully turn with wide spatula and brown other side.

Remove to warm platter and place uncovered in low oven to keep warm until sauce is finished.

Pour off excess oil from pan, being careful to save brown bits from bottom. Melt remaining butter over medium heat. Add pecans to pan and lightly toast about one minute (being careful not to burn). Deglaze pan with white wine and reduce to about 2 tablespoons.

Add cream, lemon juice, and brown sugar. Bring to a boil, reduce heat to simmer, and reduce until thickened—about 10 minutes. (When wooden spoon is dipped in sauce, draw a line with your finger across the back of the spoon. If line remains, the sauce is done.) Taste. If sauce needs more lemon juice, add to taste.

Place pike fillets on serving plates. Top with sauce. Serve with a side of rice or vegetable. Garnish with a lemon twist.

Chef's Note: This pecan sauce is very versatile. It can be used for beef tenderloin, pressed with fresh cracked black pepper; pork tenderloin; or a boneless chicken breast. Just replace pike fillets with your choice of other meat and follow above recipe. For additional flavor add a splash of Worcestershire sauce and ¼ teaspoon chopped, fresh garlic.

Yields 2 servings.

CAFE *Vienna* Of Brookfield, WI

Cafe Vienna
17700 West Capitol Drive
Brookfield, Wisconsin 53045
(414) 783-6100

Cafe Vienna was opened in 1990 as a dream of Executive Chef, Christa Wambar. She began her training in Vienna, Austria, at the Hotelfachschule and worked at the Hotel Sacher. Christa, with her husband Helmut, bring accomplished culinary artistry to Milwaukee with fine European dining at the Cafe Vienna. "Our goal is to offer the ultimate in cuisine, good service, and gracious hospitality in a carefully planned, charming atmosphere." We have found that location in the Stonewood Village complex of suburban Brookfield.

Fresh and natural ingredients are always used and prepared daily from scratch. In addition to our basic menu, we print a special daily menu for both lunch and dinner. The finest meats and vegetables are used to prepare all special culinary creations.

Reservations are recommended at the Cafe Vienna, recipient of a five-star Award of Excellence in 1991. Live piano music is featured on Friday and Saturday evenings.

Open Monday through Saturday, 11:00 a.m. to 2 p.m.
Monday through Thursday, 5:00 p.m. to 9:00 p.m.
Friday and Saturday, 5:00 p.m. to 10:00 p.m.

Major credit cards accepted

Pork Tenderloin Florentine

1 pound spinach
1 small onion
2 stalks celery
3 tablespoons oil, divided
2 eggs
½ cup grated Romano cheese
1 pork tenderloin (12 ounces), flattened ¼-inch thick
Salt and pepper to taste

Blanch spinach, rinse under cold water, squeeze dry. Dice onion, celery and spinach finely. Sauté onion and celery in 2 tablespoons oil; add spinach. Remove from heat; add eggs and grated cheese.

Spread spinach paste evenly over flattened tenderloin. Roll up lengthwise; tie with butcher string. In sauté pan over medium heat, sear tenderloin in remaining oil until all sides are browned. Bake in 350-degree oven for about 25 minutes. Salt and pepper to taste.

Slice and serve over light chicken veloute or any sauce of your choice.

Yields 2 to 3 servings.

Chancery Pub and Restaurant
Locations:
Mequon; South 27th Street, and Downer Avenue, Milwaukee; Racine; Waukesha; Wauwatosa
(414) 771-3100

The Chancery Pub has grown from a single restaurant in Racine in 1971 to six popular dining spots. Although each location is unique (such as the "tavern in the mall"), the atmosphere is always relaxed and service is friendly.

You can take your whole family and please everyone's palate with the wide selection of American and ethnic foods. Order your favorite Mexican dish, Chinese entree or the special of the day. Each location has a full bar to complement the flavors of your lunch or dinner selection.

Open Sunday through Thursday, 11 a.m. to 12 a.m.
Friday and Saturday, 11 a.m. to 1 a.m.

American Express, Visa and MasterCard accepted

Hey Curly — Where's Moe

Sweet and Spicy Sauce:
- **½ cup sugar**
- **½ cup plus 1 tablespoon soy sauce**
- **2 tablespoons sesame oil**
- **2 teaspoons Chinese chili paste with garlic**
- **½ teaspoon garlic powder**
- **1⅓ cups water**
- **2 tablespoons cornstarch**

Stir Fry:
- **8 ounces curly noodles, dry**
- **1 tablespoon vegetable oil**
- **1¼ pounds chicken, cut in small pieces**
- **1 cup zucchini, sliced**
- **4 ounces snow pea pods**
- **1½ cups broccoli buds**
- **1 medium red pepper, julienne cut**
- **1 cup carrots, julienne cut**

To make sauce combine sugar, soy sauce, sesame oil, Chinese chili paste, garlic powder and 1 cup water in a sauce pan and heat to low boiling. Mix cornstarch and remaining water and add to boiling mixture, stirring constantly. Bring back to boil for one minute. Set aside.

Prepare noodles according to package directions; do not overcook.

In a large skillet, heat oil over medium-high heat. Add chicken pieces and sauté until almost cooked, about 6 minutes. Add vegetables and continue cooking until tender crisp, about 5-7 minutes. Add Sweet and Spicy Sauce and pasta. Mix thoroughly. Heat through and serve immediately.

Yields 4 serving.

The Clock Steak House

The Clock Steak House
720 North Plankinton Avenue
Milwaukee, Wisconsin 53203
(414) 272-1278

The Kortes Family invites you to dine with us at The Clock Steak House. Our elegant decor, outstanding cuisine and ideal location make The Clock Steak House a perfect place to dine while in Milwaukee. Exceptional for either lunch or dinner, you're sure to enjoy our varied selection of steak and seafood entrees.

Open Monday through Friday, 11:30 a.m.
Saturday 4:30 p.m.

All major credit cards accepted

South of the Border Steak

4 rib eye steaks (10 ounces each)
Onion rings

Salsa:
1 tomato, seeded
1 green pepper
½ red onion
¼ cup peppercinis
½ cup olive oil
¼ cup lemon juice

Grill steaks to order. Prepare onion rings. Keep steaks and onion rings warm.

To prepare salsa, combine tomato, green pepper, red onion and peppercinis. Add olive oil and lemon juice. Top steaks with salsa and onion rings.

Yields 4 servings.

Raspberry Cheesecake

Crust:
2 cups graham cracker crumbs
½ cup sugar
¼ pound melted butter

Filling:
2¼ pounds cream cheese, softened
1 cup sugar
4 eggs
⅓ cup Chambord liqueur
½ cup raspberry preserves
2 tablespoons cornstarch
1 teaspoon vanilla
1 cup sour cream

To prepare crust, combine ingredients and pat into a 9-inch springform pan.

Combine all filling ingredients; blend until smooth. Pour into prepared crust. Bake at 325 degrees for 1¼ hours.

Yields one 9-inch cheesecake.

DICK'S BAR & GRILL ON THE ST. CROIX — HUDSON, WISCONSIN

Dick's Bar and Grill
111 Walnut Street
Hudson, Wisconsin 54016-1519
(715) 386-5222

Welcome to Dick's Bar and Grill, an establishment serving residents and travelers since 1860. Our friendly tavern, then known as the Antler Room, was founded by a local brewery and run by B. A. Smith. Shortly thereafter Smith heard the call of duty and left to fight in the American Civil War.

Through the years, several different owners have been a part of our colorful history. After WWII Dick Brunelle bought the saloon. Dick was well known throughout the valley for his generous personality and his hot dago sandwiches. Without him we wouldn't have a name for this place.

Current owner Fred Kremer bought Dick's Bar and Grill in 1982. By 1985 he had added a kitchen that would make any grandmother proud.

Today Dick's Bar and Grill is a popular meeting place. We pride ourselves in our friendly atmosphere and our unique flair. "Thanks for stoppin'." We're always pleased to welcome you!

Open 7 days a week, 8:00 a.m. to 10: p.m.

Visa, MasterCard, American Express, Diners Club accepted

Jägger Beef Goulash Soup

3 tablespoons vegetable oil
1 large sweet yellow onion, chopped
1 large green bell pepper, seeded and chopped
2 pounds top sirloin beef butt steak, trimmed and cut into ½-inch cubes
2 29-ounce cans tomatoes with juice
1 12-ounce can tomato paste
4 cups beef stock
2 cups dry white wine
2 cups water
3 potatoes, peeled and cut into ½-inch cubes
3 carrots, peeled and sliced into ½-inch pieces
3 tablespoons sweet Hungarian paprika
3 tablespoons sugar
1 teaspoon caraway seed
1 teaspoon black pepper
1 teaspoon salt
2 whole bay leaves
¼ teaspoon cayenne pepper
12 ounces dairy sour cream
Fresh minced parsley

Heat oil in a large Dutch oven or stock pot. Cook onion and green pepper for 5 minutes.

Add beef and brown on all sides. Add tomatoes, paste, stock, wine, water, potatoes, carrots, paprika, sugar, caraway seed, pepper, salt, bay leaves and cayenne pepper and bring to a boil. Reduce heat; cover and simmer for 1½ hour.

Ladle soup into large bowls. Garnish with a dollop of sour cream and sprinkle with fresh minced parsley. Serve with light and dark rye bread.

Yields 8 servings.

DICK'S SMORGASBORD

Dick's Polish-American Smorgasbord
400 County A and Highway 12
Wisconsin Dells, Wisconsin 53965
(608) 253-4451

"Delicious Homemade Cooking"

Richard and Grace Makowski emigrated from Poland in 1964 and began their business lives in Wisconsin Dells in 1971. They presently are owners of AMERICAN WORLD which consists of Dick's Polish-American Smorgasbord, American Club, Inn, Resort, Liquor Store, and Continental Motel.

Their four teenage children are active in the operation of the business.

Open seasonally May to October
Daily, 3:30 p.m. to 8:30 p.m.
Sundays and Holidays, 2:00 p.m. to 7:30 p.m.

All major credit cards accepted

Golabki

(Cabbage Rolls)

- **1 firm head of cabbage**
- **1 medium onion, chopped**
- **2 tablespoons margarine**
- **1 pound ground beef**
- **½ pound ground pork**
- **1 cup cooked short grain rice, follow package instructions**
- **Salt and pepper to taste**
- **2 eggs**
- **2 teaspoons beef stock**
- **1½ cups water**

Core cabbage and parboil one head at a time in salted water until the leaves come away easily. Remove leaves one by one and set aside to cool. When cool, cut the heavy underpart of the leaves.

Lightly brown onions with margarine. Combine uncooked beef and pork, cooked rice, salt and pepper, eggs, and beef stock. Mix until well-blended. Place desired amount of filling on the cabbage leaf and then roll the leaf.

Place cabbage rolls in 9x13-inch pan and pour 1½ cups of water over all. Cover. Cook for 1½ hours in 325-degree oven.

Yields 4-6 servings.

Fanny Hill
Restaurant, Inn & Dinner Theatre
3919 Crescent Avenue
Eau Claire, Wisconsin 54703
(715) 836-8184 (800) 292-8026

Fanny Hill Inn and Dinner Theatre, Western Wisconsin's #1 tourist attraction, has a track record for pleasing a variety of local patrons and tourists, young and old alike. The local community is usually not surprised when Fanny Hill adds yet another attraction. They have been changing, upgrading and bringing pleasure to the Chippewa Valley for 23 years.

Fanny Hill's two primary features are fine dining, awarded AAA Four Diamond Award for four consecutive years, and hilarious dinner theatre, now celebrating their 15th year of presenting live Broadway comedies.

In addition, Fanny Hill offers seven Bed & Breakfast rooms with Victorian decor, fireplaces and large whirlpools. A perfect getaway for a little R & R—Rest and Romance.

Fanny Hill's newest attractions, Grand Victorian Gardens and outdoor deck dining are sure to please those looking for a casual experience on warm summer evenings. Both the outdoor deck and gardens overlook a spectacular view of the Chippewa River Valley.

For the children, Fanny Hill changes with the seasons. Enchanting decorations and costumed characters are found at Fanny Hill throughout the year. During Christmas, The Hill becomes a wonderland with thousands of twinkling lights and a special Dinner with Santa featuring a live show with Teddy Bear and the Rockers.

During the month of October, Fanny Hill turns orange with thousands of carved pumpkins on display. Stroll the famous Halloween Hollow, a trail through the woods full of spooks and goblins. Spring and summer display the flowers and scenic beauty that surround Fanny Hill.

For a special evening of adventure any time of the year, you'll find it at the Hill—Fanny Hill.

Open Tuesday through Sunday, starting at 5:00 p.m.

Visa, Mastercard, Discover, American Express, Diners Club accepted

Pecan Creme Caramel Custard Terrine with Praline Caramel Sauce

Caramel:
- **1 cup sugar**
- **2 cups water**

Custard:
- **8 eggs**
- **1½ cups chopped pecans**
- **2 ounces Grand Marnier (orange liquer)**
- **1½ cups sugar**
- **2 teaspoons vanilla**
- **4 cups heavy cream**

Sauce:
- **1 cup sugar**
- **2 cups water**
- **¾ cup heavy cream**
- **3 ounces Praline liquer**

Prepare caramel by combining sugar and water in a thick bottom sauce pan. Boil mixture until it reaches the caramel stage (approximately 10 minutes). Watch closely or it will burn. Once caramel is formed, pull off heat immediately and pour in the bottom of a terrine mold. Allow the caramel to harden.

Preheat oven to 325 degrees. Prepare custard by combining eggs, pecans, orange liquer, sugar and vanilla. Bring cream to boil on stove and add to egg mixture stirring with a wire wisk until well combined. Pour mixture over caramel and place in a water bath; cover with parchment paper to prevent the custard from burning. Bake at 325 degrees for 45 minutes. Use a toothpick to test if it is done. If toothpick stays clean, remove custard from oven and water bath. Cool in refrigerator for 2 hours or until custard sets.

Use a sharp paring knife to cut around the outside of custard to remove it from mold. Set mold upside down on serving platter and allow custard to work its way out.

To prepare sauce, cook sugar and water on high heat and bring to caramel stage. Immediately remove from heat and whisk in cream slowly (to keep sugar from crystallizing). Add Praline liquer. Serve over custard.

Yields 8 servings.

Lowe

Quail Picou
with Cayenne Pepper Beurre Blanc

¼ cup yellow pepper, diced
¼ cup red pepper, diced
¼ cup green pepper, diced
¼ cup celery, diced
¼ cup Bermuda onion, diced
1½ tablespoons fresh, minced garlic
½ cup Andouille sausage, diced
½ cup oysters, freshly shucked
½ cup chicken stock
2 cups wild rice, cooked
¼ cup green onions, sliced
1 teaspoon fresh parsley, chopped
Salt and pepper to taste
6 quail, semi-boneless
Paprika
Thyme

Cayenne Pepper Beurre Blanc:
3 tablespoons olive oil
2 tablespoons fresh chopped garlic
2 tablespoons fresh shallots, chopped
¼ cup Andouille sausage, diced
3 sprigs fresh thyme
½ cup chicken stock
½ cup white wine
2 cups heavy whipping cream
1 pound unsalted butter, cold, cubed
1 teaspoon cayenne pepper
Salt to taste

Preheat oven to 350 degrees. Sauté peppers, celery, Bermuda onion, garlic and Andouille sausage until vegetables are soft. Add oysters and chicken stock and reduce liquid in half. Add wild rice, green onions, and parsley. Season with salt and pepper.

Let rice dressing cool and then stuff quail. Season skin of quail with salt, pepper, paprika and thyme leaves. Roast quail for 20 to 25 minutes.

To prepare beurre blanc, place olive oil in a large sauce pot. Sauté garlic, shallots and Andouille sausage about 3-5 minutes on medium heat. Add thyme, chicken stock and white wine. Reduce liquid by ⅔ on low heat. Add heavy cream and reduce on medium heat until cream starts to thicken. Once thickened, whisk in cold butter in three parts on medium heat. When butter has melted completely, immediately remove from heat and strain sauce into a serving bowl. Add cayenne pepper and salt to taste just before serving.

Serve beurre blanc with Quail Picou.

Chef's Note: If sauce is made ahead of time, keep it warm in a plastic container or else it will separate.

Yields 4-6 servings.

Fountain Blue

Fountain Blue
5133 South Lake Drive
Cudahy, Wisconsin 53110
(414) 481-1482

First opened in 1911 by Frank and Cecelia Sztukowski, the Fountain Blue Dining Room combines an elegant, comfortable atmosphere with fine cuisine. The charming brick building that was built in 1920 still houses the restaurant today.

Granddaughter Susan and her husband, Dan Nimphius, carry on the Sztukowski tradition established over eight decades ago. The restaurant was passed to the third generation from Norbert, the youngest of 19 Sztukowski children, and his wife, Rita. The fourth generation is currently learning the value of sincere hospitality.

Fountain Blue is an unpretentious restaurant combining an American menu with an ethnic flair. The Nimphius' cater from the most elegant private affairs to reasonable homecooked dinners with families in mind. It is a south side treasure with a three star rating from the Milwaukee Journal.

Just as Grandfather Frank, "The Congenial Fellow," boasted of Liberace entertaining his guests, Dan and Sue have had the honor of serving former Vice President and Mrs. Dan Quayle, "although in our eyes each and every guest is very special."

The historic Fountain Blue, with abundant stained glass windows, rich wood, running fountain and memorabilia dating back to the turn of the century, gives our patrons a feeling of yesteryear. Dining with us proves that "some of the best things never change!" In Norbie's own words, "Have a lovely!"

Open Monday through Saturday, 11 a.m. to 10 p.m.
Sunday 10:30 a.m. to 8 p.m.

All major credit cards accepted

Zupa Ogorkowa

(Polish Pickle Soup)

3 peppercorns
1 teaspoon pickling spice
2 bay leaves
3 pounds pork shanks
½ gallon water
1 potato, diced
1 small onion, diced
¼ head cabbage, coarsely chopped
½ cup pickle juice
2 Kosher dill pickles, chopped
1 teaspoon dill weed
Salt and pepper to taste

Prepare a bouquet garni by tying peppercorns, pickling spice and bay leaves in cheesecloth or coffee filter. In a medium soup kettle or Dutch oven, simmer pork shanks in water with bouquet garni until shanks are tender, approximately three hours.

Remove shanks and discard bouquet garni. Reserve pork stock. Remove meat from bone and reserve meat.

Add water to stock to make ½ gallon; add potato, onion, cabbage, pickle juice, dill pickles, dill weed, salt and pepper, and reserved meat. Simmer for one hour.

Chef's Note: Make stock one day in advance and store in refrigerator. Remove fat layer which rises to the top. Can add flavor with ham base.

Yields ½ gallon.

Friendly Inn Supper Club, Inc.
4034 West Good Hope Road
Milwaukee, Wisconsin 53209
(414) 352-2535

The Friendly Inn Supper Club, located on Milwaukee's Northwest side, was established in 1960 by owners Frank and Pauline Chlebana. This family-owned business is known for its generous portions and delicious tasting food. One of its specialties is Prime Rib, but food such as Sauerbraten, Schnitzel, various seafoods, and steaks will surely satisfy any palate. If you are in Milwaukee be sure to stop in!

Open Tuesday through Friday, 11:30 a.m. to 2:00 p.m.
Tuesday through Saturday, starting at 5:00 p.m.
Sunday starting at 4:00 p.m.

Visa, MasterCard, and American Express accepted

Sauerbraten

Sauerbraten:
- **½ cup whole mixed spices**
- **⅓ cup salt**
- **2 medium onions, sliced**
- **2 carrots, sliced**
- **Cider vinegar**
- **Water**
- **6 pounds beef, round, rump or sirloin**

Gravy:
- **8 gingersnaps**
- **2 cups hot water**
- **½ cup brown sugar**
- **½ cup red wine**
- **½ cup cider vinegar**
- **½-¾ cup flour**
- **1 stick butter**
- **Salt, to taste**
- **Black pepper, to taste**

Combine first four ingredients with a brine of one part cider vinegar and 2 parts water. Cover beef with brine mixture; store in refrigerator approximately 2 weeks, turning several times.

Discard vegetables. Drain brine, reserving for gravy if desired. Roast beef, uncovered at 325 degrees for 6 hours, or until tender.

When meat is done, place drained meat juices and fat trimmings in a medium saucepan. Add reserved brine. Dissolve gingersnaps in water and add to brine mixture. Add brown sugar, red wine and vinegar. Heat to boil. Meanwhile prepare roux by combining flour and butter in small saucepan; heat to low boil. Slowly add roux to brine mixture until desired consistency. Strain gravy through colander. Salt and pepper to taste.

Slice meat and pour hot gravy over top. Serve with Red Cabbage and Potato Dumplings.

Yields 6-8 servings.

Red Cabbage

- **4 slices bacon, chopped**
- **1 medium red cabbage, finely chopped**
- **1 tablespoon lemon juice**
- **1 medium onion, finely chopped**
- **1 medium green apple, cored and finely chopped**
- **1 cup water**
- **¼ cup apple cider vinegar**
- **¼ cup red wine vinegar**
- **¼ cup brown sugar**
- **1 teaspoon caraway seeds**
- **⅛ teaspoon ground cloves**
- **1 teaspoon salt**
- **¼ teaspoon freshly ground pepper**

Fry chopped bacon until crisp. Remove from pan, drain on paper towels; set aside.

Sauté cabbage in bacon drippings and lemon juice for 5 to 6 minutes, or until slightly limp. Add chopped onions and apples; sauté until tender.

Combine water, vinegars, brown sugar, caraway seeds, ground cloves, salt and pepper. Stir into cabbage mixture. Place mixture in casserole dish, cover and bake for 30 minutes in 350-degree oven.

Remove from oven; mix in bacon. Taste and adjust, adding more sugar or vinegar as desired. Serve with Sauerbraten and Potato Dumplings.

Yields 6-8 servings.

Potato Dumplings

12 potatoes
6 eggs
1 cup flour
1 cup bread crumbs
½ cup chopped parsley
½ cup melted butter
1 tablespoon Lawry's salt
1 tablespoon baking powder
1 box bread croutons, plain

Cook potatoes 1 day ahead with skins on. Refrigerate overnight.

Peel and shred potatoes. Combine with eggs, flour, bread crumbs, parsley, butter, salt and baking powder.

Take large tablespoon of dough in hand. Insert 1 or 2 croutons and roll dough into ball around croutons. Roll rest of dough in same manner.

Drop dumplings into pot of boiling water. Cook 3 to 4 minutes after the dumplings float.

Serve with Sauerbraten. Cover with gravy and garnish with parsley if desired.

Chef's Note: If you decide to refrigerate dumpling mixture and prepare the next day, roll dumpling in plain flour before dropping into boiling water to cook.

Yields 6-8 servings.

Wagon Trail

Resort Restaurant & Conference Center

"Overlooking Beautiful Rowley's Bay

Grandma's Swedish Restaurant
Wagon Trail Resort
1041 Highway ZZ
Ellison Bay, Wisconsin 54210
(414) 854-2385

Door County is a unique environment, recognized nationally as an ideal vacation destination. A significant part of the Door County experience is the Wagon Trail Resort & Conference Center.

Amid the many amenities Wagon Trail offers is the exquisite dining at Grandma's Swedish Restaurant & Bakery. Here "Scratch" is an operative word since all baking is done from scratch.

In the evenings, Grandma's Swedish Restaurant offers a buffet-style meal along with a selection of items from their main menu—and for those who have previously visited our facilities, we now have a new and expanded restaurant and an enlarged bakery.

When you include our conference facilities and our banquet capabilities—the Wagon Trail Resort & Conference Center is the place for you to experience Door County.

Now you can enjoy your favorite bakery items at our second location. Grandma's Swedish Bakery, at 19 Green Bay Road in Sturgeon Bay, features our renowned pecan rolls, cardamom bread and skorpa as well as assorted soups and sandwiches. Wherever you are in Door County, you're not far from your favorite from-scratch bakery at Grandma's Swedish Restaurant and Bakeries.

Open seven days a week, 7 a.m. to 9 p.m.

MasterCard, Visa, American Express and Discover accepted

Alice Peterson's Swedish Meatballs

1½ teaspoons salt
1¾ teaspoons Lawry's seasoned salt
½ teaspoon black pepper
½ teaspoon poultry seasoning
½ tablespoon Worcestershire sauce
3 pounds ground beef
1 cup chopped onions
½ cup chopped celery
2 eggs
1 cup milk
1½ cups bread crumbs

Stir salts, pepper, poultry seasoning, and Worcestershire sauce into ground beef. Mix well. Blend onions and celery with eggs in blender. Add to meat. Add milk, being careful not to pack or over mix. Add bread crumbs and toss lightly.

Roll into small balls. Place on a cookie sheet and bake until slightly browned at 350 degrees. Serve in warm, thin gravy. Freeze extra meatballs.

Chef's Note: Make a gravy by adding pan juices and water to cream of mushroom soup.

Yields 25 meatballs.

The Grandview
Restaurant & Lounge

The Grandview Restaurant & Lounge
The Geneva Inn
804 South Lake Shore Drive
Lake Geneva, Wisconsin 53147
(414) 248-5680

The Grandview Restaurant and Lounge located in The Geneva Inn has a panoramic view of Lake Geneva. The menu features American and Continental cuisine with daily fresh fish specialties.

The Geneva Inn is a relaxing retreat directly on the shores of Geneva Lake. Opened in June of 1990, most of the 37 tastefully appointed guest rooms offer vintage soaking tubs, whirlpools and private balconies.

Open daily, serving lunch, dinner and Sunday brunch

Visa, MasterCard, American Express, and Diners Club accepted

Hot Crab Dip

1 8-ounce package cream cheese, softened
½ cup sour cream
½ cup mayonnaise
1¼ teaspoons Worcestershire sauce
½ teaspoon dry mustard
Pinch garlic salt
Salt and pepper to taste
½ cup grated Parmesan cheese
½ pound lump crab meat (carefully remove cartilage)

Beat cream cheese in a mixing bowl until fluffy. Add sour cream and mayonnaise; blend well. Add Worcestershire sauce, dry mustard, garlic salt, salt and pepper; blend well. Blend in Parmesan cheese and crab meat.

Heat dip in sauce pan over low heat or in ovenproof dish in 350-degree oven.

Serve hot with herb roasted French bread cubes and freshly steamed vegetables.

Yields 3-4 cups.

Garlic Herb Butter Sauce

3 cloves garlic, finely chopped
¼ cup brandy
¼ cup heavy cream
1 pound cold butter, cut into pieces
2 tablespoons garden seasoning
Salt and pepper to taste

Sauté garlic in brandy until reduced to almost a liquid. Add cream and reduce again. Remove from heat.

Whisk in the cold butter one piece at a time. Strain sauce through a sieve. Add garden seasoning, salt and pepper.

Chef's Note: Great served with fresh walleye or grouper. If you can't find garden seasoning, use Mrs. Dash.

Yields approximately 1 cup.

Grenadier's Restaurant
747 North Broadway
Milwaukee, Wisconsin 53202
(414) 276-0747

Throughout its 18-year history, Grenadier's, a fixture on Wisconsin's fine dining scene, has transcended the state's borders to earn national recognition for its cuisine and elegant dining. Owner and chef Knut Apitz proudly attributes this deep-rooted reputation to the consistent culinary pleasures and impeccable service customers can expect at Grenadier's.

The frequently changing menu features dishes influenced by the Orient, Europe and America, all prepared with precision. The soups and desserts, too, exhibit the great pride Apitz takes in his work.

This total package of elegant dining and international cuisine have made Grenadier's one of Milwaukee's most renowned dining destinations.

Open Monday through Friday, Lunch 11:30 a.m. to 2:00 p.m.
Monday through Saturday, Dinner 5:00 p.m. to 10:30 p.m.

All major credit cards accepted

Chicken Breast with Port Wine and Whiskey Sauce

8 boneless chicken breasts, 6 ounces each
Salt and pepper to taste
Flour
2 tablespoons unsalted butter
1 tablespoon finely chopped shallots
2 tablespoons chopped walnuts
3 tablespoons whiskey
2 tablespoons port wine
5 tablespoons cream
Vegetable and pasta, for garnish.

Season chicken breasts with salt and pepper to taste. Flour lightly and sauté in butter in heated pan for 10 minutes on slow heat. Remove chicken and set on warm plate, covered to keep warm.

In the same pan, add shallots and sauté, then add the walnuts and sauté for 1 minute. Flambé the mixture with whiskey. Deglaze the pan with port wine. Add the cream and cook gently for 5 minutes.

Arrange the chicken breasts on plates and ladle sauce over them. Garnish plates to your own liking with vegetables and pasta.

Yields 8 servings.

Jack Pandl's Whitefish Bay Inn
1319 East Henry Clay Street
Whitefish Bay,
Wisconsin 53217
(414) 964-3800

Jack Pandl told us that his mother brought the recipe for German pancakes with her from the old country. It is similar to English Yorkshire puddings or popovers, in which eggs alone, hit with the sudden shock of a hot oven, perform a miraculous, high-speed leavening feat.—Jane and Michael Stern

Open Daily, 11:30 a.m. to 10:00 p.m.

All major credit cards accepted

Jack Pandl's Famous German Pancake

½ cup all purpose flour
½ cup milk
Pinch of salt
4 large eggs
1 tablespoon butter
1 tablespoon shortening
Lemon wedges
Maple syrup
Powdered sugar
Butter

Mix the flour, milk and salt together in a mixing bowl until smooth. Add the eggs and beat until smooth.

Preheat oven to 425 degrees.

Melt the butter and shortening in a 9 to 10 inch sloped-sided pan with an oven-proof handle. Pour the batter into the pan and cook on the stove until the bottom of the pancake is browned, but uncooked batter remains on top, about 2 to 3 minutes.

With a spatula, turn the pancake quickly and make a criss-cross cut all the way through the pancake. Put in preheated oven about 12 minutes or until the edges are browned. The pancake will rise 3 to 5 inches all around the edges of the pan. The criss-cross cut will close as the pancake bakes.

Remove the pancake from the oven and quickly cut into 6 servings. Serve immediately with lemon, maple syrup, powdered sugar and butter.

Yields 4 to 6 servings as a side dish, 2 servings for breakfast.

Karl Ratzsch's

THE IMPRESSIVE GERMAN RESTAURANT

Karl Ratzsch's Old World Restaurant
320 East Mason Street
Milwaukee, Wisconsin 53202
(414) 276-2720

The history of Karl Ratzsch's Restaurant goes back as far as 1904 when chef Otto Herman opened a small cafe in downtown Milwaukee. A few years later, his stepdaughter, Helen, came from Germany to live with him in quarters above the cafe.

Just prior to World War I, Karl Ratzsch Sr. took a tour of the United States and found himself stranded due to the outbreak of war. Eventually, Karl made his way to Milwaukee where he took a job at Otto Herman's Cafe. After a ten year courtship, he married Helen and bought the cafe.

In 1929, Karl and Helen relocated the business to its present location and named it The Old Heidelberg Cafe. The country was in the grip of depression during those early years, but Karl and Helen managed to establish a loyal following. Helen, affectionately known as "Mama Ratzsch", began filling the restaurant with her beautiful collection of steins, porcelain and glassware from Europe. To avoid confusion with other German restaurants, the name was changed to Karl Ratzsch's Restaurant in the early thirties.

Karl and Helen continued to be active in the operation of the restaurant throughout their years, but Karl Ratzsch Jr. took on the main responsibility late in the fifties. Under his guidance, the restaurant grew in popularity, and continues today in the traditions of quality and old world elegance established by his parents.

Open Sunday 11:00 a.m. to 9:00 p.m.
Monday through Friday, 11:30 a.m. to 10:00 p.m.
Saturday 11:30 a.m. to 10:30 p.m.

All major credit cards accepted

Swabian Veal

- **2 veal cutlets (3-ounce inside round slices), flattened to ⅛ inch**
- **Salt**
- **Black pepper, fresh-ground**
- **Flour**
- **2 tablespoons melted butter**
- **3 tablespoons diced Spanish onion**
- **1 cup veal stock**
- **2 tablespoons Burgundy wine**
- **3 tablespoons sour cream**
- **3 tablespoons heavy cream**

Heat heavy large skillet over medium high heat. Season veal cutlets with salt and fresh ground black pepper. Dredge veal in flour. Add butter and veal cutlets to skillet and sauté until cooked through and golden brown, about 1 minute per side. Transfer veal to plate, tent with foil to keep warm.

In same skillet, over medium heat, sauté diced onions for 2 minutes, slightly browning them. Deglaze with veal stock and Burgundy wine; reduce to ⅜ cup. Reduce heat to low and whisk in sour cream and heavy cream; adjust seasoning with salt and fresh ground black pepper.

Spoon sauce over veal cutlets. Serve with buttered noodles topped with poppy seeds.

Yields 2 servings.

Kavanaugh's ESQUIRE CLUB

Kavanaugh's Esquire Club
1025 North Sherman Avenue
Madison, Wisconsin 53704
(608) 249-0193

As Madison's oldest continually operated family owned restaurant, Kavanaugh's Esquire Club has long been offering food which satisfies its customers. During this time, customers of 40 years, a constant stream of new customers and an occasional past or current governor have enjoyed the food and atmosphere of Kavanaugh's.

Serving the state's capital since 1947, Kavanaugh's was one of the first to introduce a fish fry to Wisconsin. Today, with the third generation of Kavanaughs at the helm, the ever-popular fish fry is still prepared in addition to great seafood and steaks. All these favorites are served in the relaxed familiar atmosphere which continues to make Kavanaugh's Esquire Club a favorite gathering spot.

Open Monday through Friday, 11 a.m. to 2 p.m.
Monday 4 p.m. to 9 p.m. — Tuesday 4 p.m. to 9:30 p.m.
Wednesday and Thursday, 4 p.m. to 10 p.m.
Friday all day
Saturday and Sunday, 11 a.m. to 10:30 p.m.

Steak John

4 beef tenderloins (6 ounces each)
28 shrimp, peeled and deveined (21-25 count)
12 -16 large mushrooms, cleaned and sliced
3 tablespoons butter
2 tablespoons chopped garlic
12 -16 asparagus spears, cooked al dente
2 cups prepared hollandaise sauce

In a pan, over medium heat, prepare steaks to slightly underdone.

While steaks are cooking, sauté shrimp and mushrooms in butter. Add garlic and cook until shrimp are thoroughly done. Remove from heat, cover and set aside.

Place undercooked steaks in a baking dish. Top with asparagus spears, sautéed shrimp and mushrooms. Cover with hollandaise sauce. Bake at 375 degrees for 3 to 5 minutes or until steaks reach desired doneness.

Chef's Note: Prepare hollandaise recipe of your choice. Some excellent pre-made brands can be found at your grocery store.

Yields 4 servings.

King's Table Restaurant
P.O. Box 65
2717 County QQ
King, Wisconsin 54946
(715) 258-9150

Jumbo cinnamon rolls, potato pancakes, bread pudding and a full menu of breakfast, lunch and dinner foods. These can all be found at the King's Table, located in the heart of the Chain O' Lakes area and just a block from the Wisconsin Veterans Home.

Since 1977, Bill and Diane Johnson and their family have been serving guests an array of hearty and delicious foods. Visitors have been known to buy dozens of the jumbo homemade cinnamon rolls to take back home, freeze and pull out whenever they need a taste of Wisconsin. Another well-known dish is the Johnson's potato pancakes, made from scratch with potatoes grown exclusively in Waupaca County.

But the King's Table all-time customer favorite is the bread pudding. Made from homemade bread and fresh ingredients, the bread puddings are second to none.

Stop in and taste the delicious from-scratch foods and see for yourself why the King's Table is one of the area's most popular dining spots.

Open Daily, 6:30 a.m. to 10:00 p.m.

MasterCard and Visa accepted

Bread Pudding with Rum Sauce

Bread Pudding:
15 bread slices
5 cups milk
9 eggs
1 cup sugar
1½ cups raisins
2 teaspoons nutmeg

Rum Sauce:
2 cups sugar
1 cup cream
½ pound butter
2 teaspoons nutmeg
2 teaspoons rum extract

To prepare bread pudding, break up bread and put in a 9x13-inch baking pan, filling pan ¾ full.

Mix milk, eggs, and sugar and pour over bread. Sprinkle raisins and a nutmeg over top of mixture.

Place this pan in another pan containing water. Bake at 350 degrees for approximately 1 hour or until custard is firm.

To prepare rum sauce, put all ingredients in a pan; boil for 10 minutes, stirring constantly. Serve over bread pudding.

Yields 12 servings.

Mader's

Mader's Restaurant
1041 North Old World Third Street
Milwaukee, Wisconsin 53203
(414) 271-3377

Mader's world-class reputation is rooted in its humble beginnings which date back to the turn of the century when German immigrant Charles Mader put his life savings into a building at 233 West Water Street (now Plankinton Avenue). Here he opened a restaurant called "The Comfort" which served only the best food and drink—dinner with tip and beverage was $.20 and steins of "Cream City" beer were $.03 each.

"The Comfort" thrived and soon moved to its present location at 1041 North Old World Third Street. When prohibition struck in 1919, Mader turned his focus to hearty German dishes like sauerbraten, wiener schnitzel and pork shank to hold the trade without the complement of the traditional stein of beer.

By the early 30's, Mader's two sons, George and Gustave, began working in the business. When Mader died in 1938, after 36 years in business, his sons continued building the fine business.

By 1952, the Mader brothers celebrated the restaurant's 50th anniversary by adding a new dining room called "Jaeger Stube." In May of 1958, George Mader died, leaving Gus to carry on the family tradition. And by the mid 1960's, Gus' son Victor joined the business.

The 1970's brought many changes to Mader's. Katherine Mader retired after 52 years of managing the kitchen. The menu changed and evolved, and Mader's added its famous Sunday Viennese Brunch.

In the 1980's, Mader's expanded its award-winning wine list, added a gift gallery and an art gallery, added a private dining room, and remodeled other areas with panels of stained glass, huge European woodcarvings and antiques depicting Teutonic legend and history.

Today, Mader's is noted nationwide for its fine German cuisine and appears regularly on magazine lists as an outstanding restaurant. And this tradition will continue for yet another generation—Victor's daughter Kristin, and son-in-law, Roben, began restaurant management and art gallery operations in 1991.

Open Monday through Thursday, 11:30 a.m. to 10:30 p.m.
Friday through Saturday, 11:30 a.m. to 11:30 p.m.
Sunday 10:30 a.m. to 10:30 p.m.

All major credit cards accepted

Roast Duck Chambord

3 ducks, 4-4½ pound each
Salt and pepper to taste
1 quart water

Chambord Raspberry Glaze:
⅓ cup sugar
½ ounce butter
Cornstarch
Cold water
6 ounces seedless raspberry jam
3 ounces Chambord liquor
Raspberries, for garnish

Season ducks with salt and pepper. Place on rack in roasting pan. Add water. Roast breast side up at 375 degrees for 1½ hours and flip. Roast back side up for 1 hour and then flip back. Roast about 1-1¼ hours until duck is tender. Remove ducks from pan and set aside until cooled. Save remaining drippings from pan. Let drippings settle; skim fat from top and discard. The remaining drippings are the duck stock; reserve.

While duck cools, make Chambord Raspberry Glaze. Melt sugar and butter in sauce pan until it reaches caramelization. Add 1¼ cups reserved hot duck stock and stir until dissolved. Combine cornstarch and water; add to glaze to achieve medium thickness. Whip in raspberry jam and remove from heat. Add Chambord liquor. Set aside.

Split ducks, then debone by taking rib cage and wishbone out. Twist thigh bone out and twist leg bone out from the outside. Take off last joint from wing but leave wing bone in. Cut duck into four pieces and place in sauté pan. Top each piece with Chambord glaze and reduce in pan until it glazes. Add whole raspberries as a garnish. Take out of pan and place on platter. Can be served with Pecan Wild Rice, rice pilaf or your favorite wild rice recipe.

Yields 6 servings.

Pecan Wild Rice

¼ cup finely diced onions
2 ounces clarified butter
½ teaspoon marjoram leaves
½ teaspoon oregano leaves
2 cups wild rice, cooked in stock or water
¼ cup pecan pieces

Sauté onions in butter until clear; add seasonings. Add wild rice and pecans. Cook together until hot.

Can be served with Roast Duck Chambord.

Yields 6 servings.

Marc's Cafe and Coffee Mill
Marcus Restaurants, Inc.
250 East Washington Avenue
Suite 1600
Milwaukee, Wisconsin 53202-4223
(414) 223-4900

Marc's Cafe & Coffee Mill restaurants, with 13 Wisconsin locations from Kenosha to Wausau, feature an exciting new menu and an attractive, comfortable, neighborhood-oriented decor.

"Marc's Cafe & Coffee Mill offers many exciting new menu items as well as traditional favorites," said Marcus Restaurants Vice President Steve Schilling. "Our customers can enjoy their favorite meals in the new Cafe & Coffee Mill setting, which is characterized by real neighborhood pride and decor."

In addition to terrific food served by friendly staff in a pleasant environment, Schilling said, "We want each local Cafe & Coffee Mill community to 'take ownership' and feel pride in the restaurants. That's why our walls are filled with local memorabilia. We offer our customers great food served in a real neighborhood environment, filled with interesting and unique antiques, old photos, local school and Wisconsin sports items, and items shared with us by neighboring businesses and retail establishments."

The first Marc's Cafe & Coffee Mill restaurants were established in mid-1992 in the Fox River Valley and North Central Wisconsin. According to Marcus Corporation Group Vice President Bruce Olson, "The response was gratifying. As we refined our Cafe & Coffee Mill offerings, we learned that the concept was one our customers appreciated and would like to see more of."

Marc's Cafe & Coffee Mill restaurants also each feature an imported cappuccino machine, and a wide selection of gourmet and specialty coffees—available either in the restaurants, or ground or as whole beans for take-home enjoyment. Plus, the restaurants offer a tantalizing array of new desserts.

Open Sunday through Thursday, 6:00 a.m. to 11:00 p.m.
Friday and Saturday, 6:00 a.m. to 2:00 p.m.
Hours may vary, some locations open 24 hours

American Express, MasterCard, Visa, Discover accepted

Tucson Toss Salad

- **1 head romaine lettuce**
- **1 cup shredded red cabbage**
- **½ cup shredded carrots**
- **¾ cup broccoli, florets and pieces**
- **8 strips crisp bacon, cut into pieces**
- **4 grilled chicken breast, cut into chunks**
- **4 ounces croutons**
- **2 cups ranch salad dressing**
- **2 teaspoons Chef Paul Prudhomme's Blackened Redfish seasoning or any similar Cajun seasoning**
- **1 large tomato, sliced**
- **2 ounces Parmesan cheese, grated**
- **Toasted garlic bread spears or sourdough bread**

Tear romaine lettuce into bite-size pieces. Place lettuce, red cabbage, carrots, broccoli, bacon, chicken and croutons into large mixing bowl.

Ladle ranch salad dressing on salad mixture and toss ingredients together until all ingredients are coated with dressing.

Place salad into serving bowls and sprinkle seasoning evenly over salads. Shingle tomato slices on salad and sprinkle Parmesan cheese over tomatoes. Serve with sourdough or garlic bread.

Yields 4 servings.

Millie's

Millie's Restaurants
N2484 County O
Delavan, Wisconsin 53115
(414) 728-2434

Millie's Restaurants & Shopping Village was founded in September of 1964 by Mildred Novak. She and her family ran the business until 1980 when Millie turned the mantle over to her very good friend, Kitty Slater. Kitty and her family are still running the business today following the traditions established by Millie.

Millie's is located on 7 acres of rich Wisconsin farm land with lovely English gardens and a Victorian gazebo. Old fashion recipes tend to make Millie's an unforgettable experience. Each item will be served by an experienced, courteous staff member determined to make your visit most enjoyable. Enjoy the entire complex; restaurant, shops and beautifully landscaped grounds. Stop for a cocktail in the Courtyard lounge and visit one of the five gracious dining rooms where antiques abound. Following your meal, five unique boutiques, including Millie's own Gift Haus, await your browsing. Each specialty shop boasts new ideas and merchandise to fit any occasion and budget. Group tours have been enjoying the country setting for 26 years. Millie's is just 10 minutes from the Lake Geneva Kennel Club dog track and downtown Delavan and the Clown Hall of Fame.

Open January and February, Saturday and Sunday only
March through July, September through December
Tuesday through Sunday 8:00 a.m. to 4:00 p.m.
July and August, Daily

Dutch Baby Oven Pancake & Chunky Peach Sauce

Chunky Peach Sauce:
- **1 16-ounce can chunky peaches**
- **1½ teaspoons cornstarch**
- **2 tablespoons water**
- **¾ cup apricot preserves**
- **1 tablespoon butter or margarine**
- **1 cup sliced strawberries**
- **2 tablespoons brandy (optional)**

Pancake:
- **2 tablespoons butter or margarine**
- **3 eggs**
- **¾ cup all-purpose flour**
- **¾ cup milk**
- **Dash of salt**
- **Lemon wedges, for garnish**
- **Confectioner's sugar, for garnish**

To prepare Chunky Peach Sauce, first drain peaches, reserving ½ cup of the syrup. Mix cornstarch with water until smooth, then combine in a medium saucepan with reserved syrup, preserves, butter and peach chunks. Cook, stirring constantly, until mixture thickens and bubbles for 3 minutes. Remove from heat; stir in strawberry slices. Add brandy if desired. Set aside.

For pancakes, preheat oven to 425 degrees. Place butter or margarine in a shallow 2½ to 3-quart casserole or skillet with over-proof handle; set in oven for 5 minutes to melt butter and heat pan.

Meanwhile, quickly mix batter: Beat eggs in medium bowl; beat in flour until smooth. Gradually stir in milk and add salt.

Remove pan from oven, pour in batter, return to oven. Bake 20 to 25 minutes or until puffed and golden brown.

Serve at once with Chunky Peach Sauce. Lemon wedges and confectioner's sugar may be added if desired.

Yields 4-6 servings.

New Glarus Hotel
100 Sixth Avenue
New Glarus, Wisconsin 53574
(608) 527-5244

For over 18 years the New Glarus Hotel has set the standards for the best Swiss cuisine in the area. Patrons return again and again to experience both the fine food and the gemuetlichkeit of its festive Swiss atmosphere.

Enjoy authentic Swiss cuisine in our air-conditioned dining room or dine on our popular balcony overlooking downtown New Glarus. Special group and bus menus are available.

Dine and dance every Friday and Saturday night year-round to the music of the famous Roger Bright Polka Band.

The restaurant is located in downtown New Glarus—America's Little Switzerland —it's close to home, just a short drive from Madison, Chicago, and Milwaukee; but it's like taking a mini-vacation to Europe. We hope to see you soon!

Open May through October
Sunday through Thursday, 11 a.m. to 9 p.m.
November through April
Sunday through Thursday, 11 a.m. to 2 p.m. and 5 p.m. to 8 p.m.
Friday and Saturday until 10 p.m. (year-round)

MasterCard, Visa, American Express, and Discover accepted

Veal Geschnetzeltes

A Swiss National Dish

1½ pounds veal
4 tablespoons butter
3 tablespoons chopped onion
¼ cup flour
¼ teaspoon salt
¼ teaspoon pepper
¼ teaspoon paprika
1 cup dry white wine
¾ cup sour cream
1 tablespoon chopped parsley

Trim the meat of all fat and gristle. Cut against the grain into strips ¼ to ½ inch wide and 1 inch long.

Heat the butter in a large skillet. Add the onions and cook 3 minutes, or until soft and golden. Add the veal. Cook, stirring constantly for 3 minutes.

Sprinkle the flour over the veal. Stir in the salt, pepper and paprika; add the wine and the sour cream. Cook over low heat, stirring constantly, until the mixture comes just below the boiling point and thickens.

Sprinkle with chopped parsley. Serve immediately.

Yields 4 servings.

The Norske Nook

In the ♥ of Osseo

"Home Cookin' At Its Best"

The Norske Nook
207 West 7th Street
Osseo, Wisconsin 54758
(715) 597-3069

Owner Jerry Bechard and his staff invite you to the Norske Nook in downtown Osseo, Wisconsin, located 20 miles south of Eau Claire on Interstate 94.

When Jerry bought the restaurant in 1990, he vowed he would not change the old-fashioned home cooking and friendly hometown service the Norske Nook customers had come to expect.

It looks like he succeeded admirably! The 1992 Wisconsin Trails Magazine readers' poll named the Norske Nook the best unusual or ethnic restaurant in the state, and the 1993 poll decided that the Norske Nook made the best desserts in the state.

Jane and Michael Stern's 1992 Roadfood Book declared that the Norske Nook was "one of the great gastronomical magnets of the midwest."

Coming in early 1994, our new bakery just across the street will be open for business.

Open Monday through Saturday, 5:30 a.m. to 9:30 p.m.
Memorial Day through Labor Day, Sunday 8 a.m. to 4 p.m.

Sour Cream Blueberry Apple Pie

2 cups sour cream
4 egg yolks
1¾ cups sugar
4 heaping teaspoons flour
1½ cups finely chopped McIntosh apples
2 cups wild Maine blueberries
1 baked single 10-inch crust
2 cups whipped whipping cream

Stir the sour cream and egg yolks together in a heavy saucepan. Add the sugar, flour and chopped apples and mix. Cook over medium heat until the filling is glossy and thick (about 5 minutes after a full boil). Add the cleaned blueberries. Let cool and pour into cool crust.

Let cool completely; then add whipped topping.

Yields 8 servings.

Old Rittenhouse Inn
Jerry and Mary Phillips, Innkeepers
301 Rittenhouse Avenue
Bayfield, Wisconsin 54814
(715) 779-5111

Elegant Victorian lodging and dining in quaint village overlooking the Apostle Islands National Lakeshore. Twenty guest rooms, among three Victorian homes, are each furnished with antiques, fireplaces and private baths. Six course gourmet dinners, featured in Gourmet *magazine, change daily to utilize the area's fresh fruit and fish. This recipe is included in the Inn's premiere cookbook entitled "Favorite Recipes from the Old Rittenhouse Inn."*

Open May through October, Dinner
November through April, Weekends only
Year around lodging

Visa, MasterCard accepted

Strawberry Consommé

2 cups strawberry juice
2 cups cranberry juice
1 cup apple juice
¾ cup sugar
⅛ teaspoon ground cardamom
⅛ teaspoon ground coriander
½ cup dry red wine
½ cup club soda
8 strawberries stemmed and sliced, for garnish
Fresh mint leaves, for garnish

Combine strawberry juice, cranberry juice, apple juice, sugar, cardamom and coriander. Bring to a boil.

Remove from heat. Stir in red wine.

Just before serving, add club soda. Garnish with sliced, stemmed strawberries and mint leaves. May be served hot or chilled.

Chef's Note: It's very easy to make strawberry juice. Simply bring 1 quart of crushed fresh berries to boil in a saucepan with 2 cups of cold water. Reduce heat and simmer for 30 minutes. Strain strawberry pulp, return juice to sauce pan, and reduce to 2 cups liquid.

Yields 8 servings.

Pasta! basta!
2336 North Farwell
Milwaukee, Wisconsin 53211
(414) 278-8050

In Italian, basta means "that's it, that's all." The chefs at Pasta!basta!, owner Bruno Kaiser and his son, do just as the name suggests—specialize in making pastas and sauces. And there dedication shows in the foods they prepare. Earning three and one-half stars from Milwaukee Journal food critic Dennis Getto and other awards such as Best Pasta and Best Carry-out and Delivery Food, Pasta!basta! has become well-known in the area for its innovative food and convenient service.

An abundance of flavorful and diverse sauces, from marinara to alfredo, are offered, many infused with seasoned butters for additional flavor. All dishes are made as ordered to ensure freshness and served to the customer at the peak of perfection.

Lunch, Monday through Friday, 11 a.m. to 2 p.m.
Dinner, Sunday through Thursday, 5 p.m. to 9 p.m.
Friday and Saturday, 5 p.m. to 10 p.m.

MasterCard, Visa and American Express accepted

Linguine with Artichokes and Goat Cheese

1½ pound linguine
2-3 ounces olive oil
16 whole artichoke hearts, quartered
8 ounces sun-dried tomatoes, soaked and cut into strips
2 ounces crushed garlic
1 pound goat cheese, crumbled
Pepper to taste
Parsley, chopped, for garnish

Cook linguine according to directions on package. While linguine is cooking, put 2 to 3 ounces of olive oil in frying pan over medium heat. Add quartered artichokes and tomatoes and heat through.

When linguine is done, drain and add to artichoke and tomato mix. Add crushed garlic and crumbled goat cheese. Heat and mix thoroughly.

Divide onto four plates. Garnish with pepper and parsley.

Chef's Note: No salt is required due to the sharpness of the cheese and the acidity of the tomatoes. Very fast and easy to prepare.

Yields 4 servings.

The Pfister
MILWAUKEE'S PREFERRED HOTEL

The Pfister Hotel
The Cafe at the Pfister
424 East Wisconsin Avenue
Milwaukee, Wisconsin 53202
(414) 273-8222

Discover all the charm of a Parisian sidewalk cafe, just a few steps into the Pfister. Alabaster lamps, fresh flowers and wrought iron columns welcome guests to this classic "bistro" atmosphere, perfect for a light snack or breakfast, pleasant dinner or lunch, served to your liking (and schedule).

Open 6 a.m. to 11 p.m.

All major credit cards accepted

Grilled Tuna Nicoise

Roasted Red Onion Vinaigrette:
- **8 ounces red onions**
- **1 cup olive oil**
- **¼ cup honey**
- **1 cup red wine**
- **½ cup cider vinegar**
- **⅛ cup minced shallots**
- **Salt and pepper**

Grilled Tuna Nicoise:
- **6 handfuls of a mixture of radicchio, frisee, red leaf romaine lettuces**
- **6 tuna steaks, skin off, 5 ounces each**
- **1 cup asparagus tips, blanched**
- **3 hard boiled eggs, cut into 6 segments**
- **18 small red potatoes, roasted**
- **½ cup fresh chives, ½-inch long**
- **1 cup diced tomatoes**

To prepare onion vinaigrette, place sliced red onions, oil, half of honey and red wine in a large skillet over medium heat. Stir frequently. Cook until onions are tender and caramelized.

Puree onion mixture. Whip remaining vinaigrette ingredients into the onion puree and rectify seasoning. Put in squeeze bottle and serve at room temperature.

To prepare tuna nicoise, first cut, clean, and dry all lettuces. Arrange them on a large plate.

Grill the tuna steak to medium. Slice the tuna ⅛-inch thick and lay on lettuces. Arrange asparagus, eggs and potatoes around tuna. Finish presentation with chives and tomatoes.

Serve immediately to enjoy hot tuna on crispy lettuces. Add onion dressing from squeeze bottle.

Yields 6 servings.

The Pfister

MILWAUKEE'S PREFERRED HOTEL

The Pfister Hotel
The English Room
424 East Wisconsin Avenue
Milwaukee, Wisconsin 53202
(414) 273-8222

The Pfister's rich tradition of fine dining is captured and preserved in the English Room. Amid warm, inviting surroundings, a select array of delicious cuisine awaits. Traditional favorites, flavorful new dishes, or your own four-course creation, from our Prix Fixe menu.

Open 11:30 a.m. to 2:00 p.m., 5:00 p.m. to 11:00 p.m.

All major credit cards accepted

Grilled Smoked Duck Breast "Silverado"

Raspberry Champagne Vinaigrette:
- **3 ounces raspberry puree**
- **1 ounce raspberry vinegar**
- **⅛ cup olive oil**
- **½ cup white wine**

Grilled Duck:
- **6 grilled smoked duck breasts, 4 ounces each, julienned**
- **½ cup toasted pine nuts**
- **1 large red bell pepper, julienned**
- **1 large green bell pepper, julienned**
- **1 large yellow bell pepper, julienned**
- **1 red onion, julienned**
- **1 package enoki mushrooms, trimmed to 2 inches**
- **2 cups fresh spinach chiffonade**
- **6 ounces fiddlehead ferns, blanched**
- **12 ounces baby lettuce**

Prepare raspberry vinaigrette by whisking ingredients together.

Marinate the duck breast, nuts, peppers, onion, mushrooms, spinach chiffonade and fiddleheads in vinaigrette, in refrigerator, for at least one hour. On serving plates, arrange marinated ingredients on evenly distributed baby lettuce.

Refrigerate until serving time.

Chef's Note: To chiffonade spinach, tightly roll leaves then slice roll in uniform thin ribbons.

Yields 6 servings.

Polecat & Lace

Polecat & Lace
West Side on Main
Minocqua, Wisconsin 54548
(715) 356-3335

As you're traveling northern Wisconsin for the fishing, the hunting, the snowmobling or the relaxation, be sure to stop by Polecat & Lace in Minocqua. Whether you're a summer traveller stopping in for a piece of homemade pie and a cool drink or a winter outdoor enthusiast in to warm up with a bowl of homemade soup, you'll feel welcome at Polecat & Lace.

The family owned and operated restaurant and pub, with its warm wood interior, casual atmosphere, daily specials, and full bar, is a relaxed and friendly place for you to spend your days of leisure.

This Chicken Fettuccine recipe is submitted in memory of Chef Chuck Hennen.

Open 7 days a week except Labor Day to Memorial Day, closed Sunday
Serving from 11:00 a.m.

MasterCard and Visa accepted

Chicken Fettuccine

4 boneless chicken breasts (4 ounces each)
3 tablespoons melted butter
1 cup Chablis wine
2 tablespoons chopped green onion
1 teaspoon basil pesto
¼ cup black olives
1 clove fresh garlic, chopped
1⅓ cups fresh mushrooms
3 cups heavy cream
1 cup grated Romano cheese
1 pound fettuccine, cooked
1 tomato, chopped

Cut chicken breasts into strips and sauté in butter. Add Chablis, onion, pesto, olives, garlic, and mushrooms. Simmer 3 to 4 minutes. Add cream, bring to a boil and add Romano cheese. Cook until sauce thickens. Add fettuccine and tomatoes. Cook 3 minutes. Serve immediately.

Chef's Note: If sauce is too thick, add additional cream.

Yields 4 servings.

Quivey's Grove
6261 Nesbitt Road
Madison, Wisconsin 53719
(608) 273-4900

Quivey's Grove is located on five acres of trees, gardens, and lawn, two miles south of Madison. It has two distinctive restaurants located in stone buildings dating from 1855 and listed on the National Register of Historic Places.

The Stone House is the refurbished residence of John Mann, who traded the lumber from his property to obtain stone from the quarry across the road. Today there is fine dining in the old bedrooms and parlors, restored with antiques, artwork from the period, and beautiful handmade quilts from the 1800's hanging on the wall. Wisconsin regional cuisine is featured with entrees named for people from Wisconsin's colorful past.

Connected by the underground tunnel is the Stable Grill, located in the restored stone and handhewn beam horse stable. In 1979 the horses and hay from the three-level loft were removed, the south facing gable end was filled with glass to provide a bright dining area upstairs, and a 40 foot brass bar with eleven Wisconsin beers on tap was installed. Today, entrees named after the local farming communities and towns feature ribs, cornish hen, smoked pork loins, and prime rib from the outdoor smoke roaster, and steaks, fish, and chicken from the grill. Casual dining in the finest Wisconsin tradition.

When in the area, Quivey's Grove is always worth a stop because as their motto says "Other restaurants are in Wisconsin, Quivey's Grove is Wisconsin."

Open Daily, 11 a.m. to 2:30 p.m. and 5 p.m. to 10 p.m.

MasterCard and Visa accepted

Quivey's Sautéed Veal and Smoked Pork

with Parsley Cream on Potato Cakes with Asparagus

Asparagus:
24 medium asparagus

Parsley Cream Sauce:
1 bunch parsley
1 cup wild mushrooms, finely diced
½ cup leek, finely diced
2 tablespoons butter, clarified
1 clove garlic, minced
2 cups cream
2 tablespoons Madeira wine
Salt and pepper to taste

Potato cakes:
½ cup onion, diced
3 tablespoons butter
1 teaspoon salt
½ teaspoon black pepper
¾ cup half and half cream
1 pound potatoes, shredded
2 ounces Parmesan cheese
2 eggs
1 cup bread crumbs
3 tablespoons butter, clarified

Wash asparagus well. Cut off tough fibrous ends. Steam over boiling water to crisp tender. Plunge into cold water to stop cooking. Trim to uniform 4-inch length. Slice trimmings into rounds and reserve to go with the veal.

Remove stems from parsley and blanch in a small amount of water for three minutes. Drain and cool. Squeeze out all water. Sauté the mushrooms and leek in the butter on high heat until soft. Add the garlic, lower the heat and cook one minute. Add half the cream, raise the heat and boil vigorously until very thick. Add remainder of cream and boil until coats a spoon heavily. Add the parsley and warm for 2 minutes, breaking up the parsley. Add the Madeira wine. Add salt and pepper to taste. Hold warm.

In heavy pot, sauté onions in butter for 3 to 4 minutes, adding salt, pepper and cream. Bring to boil, add potatoes and reduce heat. Cook, stirring occasionally until the cream thickens with the potato starch. Add Parmesan cheese and cool. Add eggs and mix. Form into 4 equal cakes about ½ inch thick. Coat with bread crumbs. Sauté in clarified butter in hot pan until brown on one side. Turn and lower heat to cook through. Place in warm oven to hold while preparing veal.

Continued on page 84.

Continued from page 82.

Veal:
- **12 ounces veal round**
- **4 ounces smoked pork loin**
- **4 large shiitake mushroom caps**
- **4 cloves garlic**
- **¼ teaspoon salt**
- **2 tablespoons butter, clarified**
- **¼ cup leek, julienned**
- **Fresh parsley, for garnish**

Slice veal and pork into ¼ inch strips. Slice mushroom caps into strips. Smash garlic with salt and reserve.

Sauté the veal in butter in a hot pan for 3 minutes. Add the pork, garlic, mushrooms, leeks, and reserved asparagus slices and sauté 2 minutes. Add half the parsley cream to the pan and stir to coat; heat through. Reserve.

Coat plates with 2 ounces of parsley cream each. Warm asparagus spears and arrange as spokes on each plate. Top with potato cake. Top potato cake with veal mixture and garnish with fresh parsley.

Yields 4 servings.

Rock Garden Supper Club
1951 Bond Street
Green Bay, Wisconsin 54303
(414) 497-4701

The Rock Garden has been a family business since 1978. We currently have 140 seats in our dining room which serves luncheons daily and a varied menu seven days a week. Our banquet rooms have seating for 1000 people in various rooms.

Open 7 days a week
Lunch, except Saturday, 11:00 a.m. to 2:00 p.m.
Dinner Monday through Thursday, 5:00 p.m. to 10:00 p.m.
Friday and Saturday, 5:00 p.m. to 11:00 p.m.
Sunday 5:00 p.m. to 9:00 p.m.

All major credit cards accepted

Danish Puff Pastry

Crust:

1 cup butter
2 cups flour
4 tablespoons water

Filling:

2 cups water
1 cup butter
2 cups flour
6 eggs
2 teaspoons vanilla
Frosting
Nuts

Combine butter, flour, and water for crust. Divide in half. Press dough out by hand to make two 8-inch circles. Place on cookie sheet.

Bring water and butter for filling to a boil. Remove from heat and add flour. Stir lightly. Add eggs and vanilla all at once. Mix ingredients just until combined. Do not overmix. Return to low heat for approximately one minute.

Spread filling on crusts. Bake at 400 degrees for 30 minutes. Cool. Frost and top with nuts.

Yields 2 8-inch pastries.

Steamboat Inn
307 Lake Street North
Prescott, Wisconsin 54021
(715) 262-8232

Our delicious Turtle Pie recipe was published in the November 1990 issue of Bon Appetit.

Open Monday through Friday, 11:30 a.m. to 2:00 p.m.
Monday through Saturday, 4:30 p.m. to 10:00 p.m.
Sunday 12:00 to 9:00 p.m.

American Express, Discover, Visa and MasterCard accepted

Steamboat Inn Turtle Pie

18 chocolate wafer cookies (about 4 ounces)
¼ cup (½ stick) unsalted butter, melted
1 cup chocolate fudge topping
6 cups pecan-praline ice cream, softened
½ cup butterscotch sauce
½ cup chopped pecans
Whipped cream

Finely grind cookies in processor. Transfer to bowl. Mix in melted butter. Press crumbs into 9-inch diameter pie dish. Freeze until cold, 20 minutes.

Spread chocolate fudge topping evenly over bottom of crust. Spoon ice cream over. Smooth top. Freeze until firm, at least 4 hours or overnight.

Spread butterscotch sauce over ice cream. Sprinkle with pecans. Spoon whipped cream into pastry bag fitted with medium star tip. Pipe cream decoratively around edge of pie and serve.

Yields 8 servings.

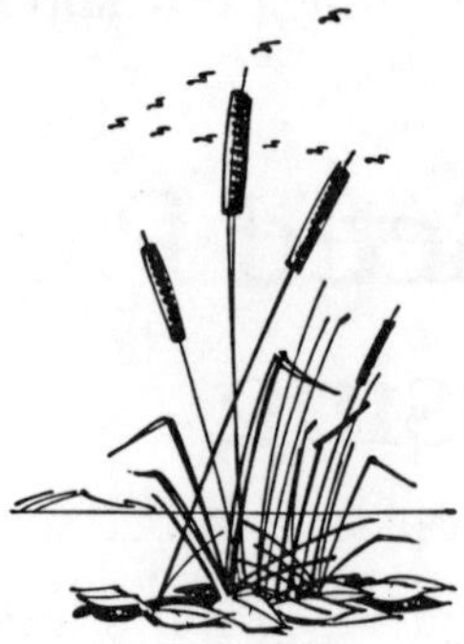

Tailgate Resort Motel
Mountain, Wisconsin 54149
(715) 276-7200

The Tailgate Restaurant was purchased by Ron and Lillian Heuser in 1977. The restaurant features Ron's daily homemade specials at breakfast, lunch and dinner.

The Tailgate was expanded to seat 50 people in 1978 and a gift shop was opened in 1988.

Ron and Lillian and staff are very proud of their involvement in the WRA and credit the association with help in making their operation a success.

Open 7 days a week
Serving from 6:00 a.m.
Closed Christmas Day

Ron's Celery Seed Coleslaw Dressing

3 cups oil
½ cup white vinegar
1½ cups white sugar
1 tablespoon horseradish
½ teaspoon salt
¼ cup grated onion
2¼ teaspoons whole celery seed

Combine oil and vinegar. In a large bowl, add all ingredients alternately except celery seed, starting with and ending with oil. Add slowly and mix thoroughly between each addition.

When ingredients are mixed completely, stir in whole celery seed.

Chef's Note: Also good served on chicken salad and some fruit salads.

Yields approximately 4 cups.

the thym's

Thym's Supper Club
Highway 23 North
Dodgeville, Wisconsin 53533
(608) 935-3344

This recipe has been used by Thym's for 29 years and still is a statewide favorite. So many people have asked for our recipe, but we have not given it out until now.

We produce approximately 1½ tons of this dip each year for our salad bar and special functions.

At one time, Thym's manufactured this product and sold containers of the Veggie Dip to many prominent grocery stores and cheese shops across the state. Because of its demand, we are considering getting back into the manufacturing process.

This will be the first and last time that Thym's will publish the recipe for this extremely simple but unbelievably popular dip.

A word to the wise though; use only the highest quality ingredients possible. Without doing this, do not expect to produce the highest demand.

Open Monday through Friday, 11:00 a.m. to 10:00 p.m.
Saturday 5:00 p.m. to 10:00 p.m.
Sunday 10:30 a.m. to 9:00 p.m.

All major credit cards accepted

Thym's Veggie Dip

1 pound cream cheese
1 teaspoon freeze-dried chives
Pinch garlic powder
1 teaspoon granulated chicken base
4 tablespoons whole milk

Combine all ingredients in 2½ quart mixer. Using electric beater, whip until completely mixed and smooth (approximately 3 minutes at high speed).

Stored in refrigerator, dip will hold for 3-4 weeks. Best eaten at slightly below room temperature.

Chef's Note: Have plenty of fresh vegetables and crackers available—this will go fast!

Yields 3 cups.

TrimB's
201 South Walnut
Appleton, Wisconsin 54911
(414) 734-9204

Ron and Carol Trimberger bought Bleier's restaurant 20 years ago. Rocky Bleier, the famous football and Vietnam war hero of the Pittsburgh Steelers, tended bar for his Dad at Bleier's.

TrimB's has constantly grown and expanded to be one of the largest and busiest restaurants in the Fox Valley area. Over 25 gallons of TrimB's famous Wisconsin Cheddar Cheese soup is served every week.

Open Monday through Friday, 11 a.m. to 10 p.m.
Saturday and Sunday, 4 p.m to 10 p.m.

All major credit cards accepted

Cheddar Cheese Soup

- **2 tablespoons finely diced onion**
- **2 tablespoons finely diced celery**
- **2 tablespoons finely diced carrots**
- **¼ cup butter**
- **¼ cup flour**
- **6 cups chicken stock**
- **2 cups scalded milk**
- **2 cups grated cheddar cheese**
- **Salt and pepper**

Sauté the onions, celery, and carrots in butter until tender; add the flour, and blend well with a wooden spoon. Add the stock slowly, stirring constantly. Simmer a few minutes.

Add the milk and cheese and season with salt and pepper to taste. Heat until the cheese is melted.

Soup can be kept warm in baine marie until serving time.

Chef's Note: For an added crunch, garnish this soup with popcorn.

Yields 12 servings.

2510 Restaurant
2510 Stewart Avenue
Wausau, Wisconsin 54401
(715) 845-2510

The 2510 Restaurant and Deli/Bakery is an evolution of over 20 years of restaurant ownership by Pat and Sue Baumer. Their concept of food and hospitality has taken this restaurant to a ranking of 248th in the Restaurant Hospitality's Top 500 Independent Restaurants in the country.

2510 prides itself in the ability to satisfy all diners. Freshly made bread, soups, and an array of salads prepared daily in the Deli/Bakery complement a vast lunch and dinner menu offering varieties from burgers to Lobster and Steaks cut daily.

The guests of 2510 have enjoyed many renovations over the years. The original restaurant was only one-third the size of the present operation. Currently there are plans for future expansion. Due to the tremendous growth in the Deli/Bakery and Carry-out Business, the expansion plans will focus in these two areas.

All of the growth and change has been a tremendous challenge to the management and staff; challenges that have been met with enthusiasm and excitement. 2510 thrives on being on the cutting edge of the hospitality industry and will always reach out to this ever-changing market!

Open Daily 11:00 a.m. to 10:00 p.m.

MasterCard, Visa, American Express, Discover accepted

Potato Cheese Soup

2½ cups diced carrots
1⅓ cups diced celery
3 tablespoons diced onions
1½ teaspoons white pepper
⅛ teaspoon black pepper
11 cups chicken broth
11 tablespoons melted butter
¾ cup white flour
4 cups milk
1 cup shredded cheddar cheese
3 cups potatoes, cooked, peeled, and diced into 1-inch squares
Shredded cheese, for garnish
Bacon bits, for garnish

In a large soup pot, bring all vegetables, seasonings, and chicken broth to a slow boil. Cook until all vegetables are tender.

Meanwhile make a roux by heating butter and flour over medium heat until thickened, stirring constantly. Remove from heat and set aside.

Add milk, cheese, and potatoes to vegetable mixture. Bring back to the verge of boiling.

Whip in roux, adding only a small amount at a time until the consistency is creamy and smooth.

Garnish with additional shredded cheese and bacon bits before serving.

Yields 18-20 servings.

THE VALLEY INN

The Valley Inn
105 Walnut Street
Neenah, Wisconsin 54957
(414) 725-8441

The Fox Valley's business and vacation travelers always look forward to a trip through Neenah and a stay at the Valley Inn. Its restful accommodations, fine American cuisine and excellent service have earned the Valley Inn several hospitality awards and meeting planner awards since the resort was built in 1966.

Diners at the Valley Inn restaurant enjoy chef Jeff Horejs' Door County Cherry Chicken and other regional specialties. And a meal there would not be complete without a delicious dessert or at least one of the popular chocolate chip cookies, baked fresh daily.

With its large banquet and meeting facilities, full service catering and courteous staff, the Valley Inn has become one of the Fox Valley's premier hotels for business meetings and travelers.

Open Daily

All major credit cards accepted

Valley Inn Door County Chicken

⅓ cup flour
½ teaspoon paprika
¼ teaspoon salt
¼ teaspoon white pepper
1 chicken breast split, skinned and boned (5-6 ounces each half)
4 ounces clarified butter or margarine
½ cup cherry juice
3 tablespoons whipping cream
1½ teaspoons sugar
½ teaspoon lemon juice
1 tablespoon cornstarch
1 tablespoon water
20 frozen, tart cherries, thawed
1 cup cooked rice (white and wild)
1 teaspoon sliced almonds
Fresh parsley, chopped, for garnish

Combine flour, paprika, salt and pepper. Dredge chicken in flour mixture; sauté in butter or margarine over medium heat until cooked through, 8 to 10 minutes. Remove from pan and keep warm.

Add cherry juice and cream to pan. Cook for 3 to 4 minutes over medium heat or until liquid is reduced by half. Add sugar and lemon juice. Combine cornstarch and water; add to cream mixture, a little at a time, until sauce is desired consistency. Add cherries, simmer 2 minutes.

Arrange rice on plates with chicken breasts. Pour sauce over chicken. Top with almonds and parsley.

Yields 2 servings.

Weissgerber's Third Street Pier
1110 N. Old World 3rd St.
Milwaukee, Wisconsin 53203
(414) 272-0330

"Milwaukee's Finest Riverfront Restaurant"

Our family is very fortunate and proud to have shared, at least in a small way, in the American Dream, starting with nothing and accomplishing more than we had dared to hope for. Since settling in the Milwaukee area in 1956, arriving here from the Black Forest area of Germany, Hans and Maria Weissgerber, Sr. opened the first family-owned and operated Golden Mast Restaurant on Okauchee Lake in the summer of 1967. After both sons, Hans Jr. and Jack, completed their education, military service and enjoyed professional employment in industry, they too joined the family restaurant. Both contributed continual growth resulting in two additional restaurants in the Waukesha County area—the Seven Seas on Nagawicka Lake, and the Gasthaus Inn in Waukesha.

The Third Street Pier and our participation in the Edelweiss Luxury Tour Boats on the Milwaukee River reflect our latest effort to provide our many and loyal customers with a new dimension in elegant dining. Experience great food and service with the most dramatic views of Milwaukee's new and exciting downtown.

We are grateful for your loyal support and invite you to enjoy fine dining in the Weissgerber tradition.

Open Monday through Friday,
Lunch 11:30 a.m. to 2:00 p.m., Dinner 5:00 p.m. to 10:00 p.m.
Saturday Dinner 5:00 p.m. to 10:00 p.m.
Sunday Dinner 4:00 p.m. to 9:00 p.m.

American Express, Visa, MasterCard, Discover accepted

Chocolate Pecan Pie

1¼ cups light corn syrup
½ cup sugar
3 ounces chocolate chips
1 teaspoon vanilla
½ cup evaporated milk or heavy cream
3 eggs, beaten
1 cup pecans
1 9-inch pie shell, unbaked
4 cups real whipped cream

Heat corn syrup, sugar, chocolate chips, vanilla and evaporated milk just until the chocolate melts. Add beaten eggs.

Pour pecans into pie shell. Add heated mixture to pie shell. Bake at 350 degrees for 50 to 60 minutes until set. Cool.

After cooling, top with the whipped cream.

Chef's Note: Place pie on sheet pan to catch drips during baking.

Yields 1 9-inch pie.

Frozen Peanut Butter Pie

20 ounces Oreo cookies, crushed
⅓ cup melted butter
28 ounces crunchy peanut butter (about 3 cups)
2 cups sugar
1 pound cream cheese, room temperature
16 ounces Cool Whip topping
Whipped cream, for garnish
Chocolate sauce, for garnish

Combine cookies and butter, and press into two greased pie pans. Freeze while making filling.

For filling, blend peanut butter, sugar and cream cheese in an electric mixer; fold in Cool Whip. Pour into the two pie pans. Freeze.

Serve garnished with whipped cream and chocolate sauce drizzled over the top.

Yields 2 9-inch pies.

Western Lakes Golf Club
W287 N1963 Oakton Road
Pewaukee, Wisconsin 53072
(414) 691-0900

Western Lakes Golf Club offers the finest in dining and banquet facilities, served in a relaxing atmosphere with spectacular views of both the countryside, and our beautifully manicured 18-hole championship golf course.

Western Lakes was built in 1963 and was formerly called Tumblebrook Country Club. Gary and Maureen Monfre and Greg and Paula Essig purchased the facility in 1988. The name was then changed to Western Lakes Golf Club to show location and geographic features of this area. We are west of the Milwaukee area and also located in a heavily populated lake area.

Western Lakes, where a truly professional staff, and a spectacular setting combine to create an atmosphere of success for your next meeting, wedding, banquet or other special event. Our elegant rooms are an enticing setting for banquets hosting 40 to 300 guests.

We hope you will enjoy our special Chicken Cordon Bleu recipe, and we look forward to serving you at Western Lakes Golf Club!

Open Monday through Sunday, 9 a.m. to 10 p.m.
Friday Fish Fry
Sunday Brunch

MasterCard, Visa accepted

Chicken Cordon Bleu

- **4 boneless, skinless chicken breasts, 8-ounces each**
- **5 ounces shaved smoked ham (4 1.25-ounce slices)**
- **4 ounces grated Swiss cheese (4 1-ounce portions)**
- **1¼ tablespoons butter**
- **1¼ tablespoons flour**
- **1½ cups hot milk**
- **1 ounce Swiss cheese, grated**
- **2 tablespoons Parmesan cheese**
- **⅛ teaspoon white pepper**
- **1½ tablespoons Rhine wine**
- **¼ teaspoon salt**

Pound breasts out to uniform thickness of about ¼-inch. Lay equal amounts of ham on each breast. Top each breast with equal amounts of cheese. Roll up each breast, folding in sides. Place in a shallow roasting pan, seam side down. Bake covered at 350 degrees for 25 to 35 minutes.

Meanwhile, make Mornay sauce. Combine butter and flour in medium sauce pan. Cook about 1 minute over medium heat. Add hot milk and whisk until smooth. Add remaining ingredients and whisk until smooth. Keep warm.

When breasts are done, ladle sauce over chicken and serve immediately.

Chef's Note: Do not overcook the chicken. This will cause the cheese to run out. Serve with wild rice and fresh asparagus.

Yields 4 servings.

Index

K

L

M

N

O

P